HOW
LINCOLN
Became President

LINCOLN IN 1860.

HOW
LINCOLN
Became President

The Part Played by BLOOMINGTON, *Illinois and Certain of its Citizens in Preparing Him for the Presidency and Securing His Nomination and Election*

By SHERMAN DAY WAKEFIELD

Illustrated from Contemporary Prints and Photographs

New York
Wilson-Erickson Inc.
1936

PRINTED IN THE UNITED STATES OF AMERICA
BY THE COLONIAL PRESS INC., CLINTON, MASS.

TO

JESSE W. FELL

DAVID DAVIS

AND

LEONARD SWETT

IN GRATITUDE FOR THE GIFT OF

ABRAHAM LINCOLN

INTRODUCTION

I HAVE known the author of this book since his early childhood. His parents and grandparents on both his maternal and paternal sides were my close friends. Sherman D. Wakefield was born and grew to manhood in Bloomington, Illinois, where as a young boy, he heard stories about the great Lincoln and his association with the life and men of this prairie town. His grandfather, Dr. Cyrenius Wakefield, was a warm and trusted friend of Abraham Lincoln in the days when Davis, Swett and Lincoln rode the old Eighth Circuit.

The influences into which Sherman D. Wakefield was born have helped to qualify him for the important task he has here achieved. The pages of this book cover a period in the life of Lincoln and important events that no other historian has adequately developed. For this reason, and for its scholarly attainments, this book will be accepted as a valuable contribution to the Lincoln history.

It was my good fortune to see Lincoln many times in Court and to hear him deliver one of his greatest speeches. I knew David Davis, Leonard Swett and Jesse W. Fell as intimate friends and neighbors. The author has done full justice to a so-far neglected phase of the life of the Great

Emancipator, and admirers of Lincoln will read
these pages with interest and profit. For surely
Lincoln was the greatest man of his century. His
lasting fame will forever rest upon the statesman-
ship and courage displayed in his effort to preserve the Federal Union.

It was in Bloomington, from his devoted
friends Davis, Swett and Fell, that Lincoln received in great part the inspiration and gained the
fortitude to stand firm and steadfast through the
struggle. Many another star rose and set in the
great conflict, but his burned with an ever-increas-
ing luster to the last. Great, serene and steadfast
a statesman and yet one of the people, trusting
only God more than the people, Lincoln seized the
helm of State in the darkest hour this nation ever
saw, and left it in the dawn of a resplendent glory
to lie down weary and broken beneath a monument of public gratitude, the greatest and most
enduring that marks the grave of mortal man.

Bloomington, Illinois.

Joseph W. Fifer

LIST OF ILLUSTRATIONS

AUTHOR'S NOTE

NO American has been more discussed and written about than has Abraham Lincoln. Every year sees new books and articles describing some phase of his ancestry, life or character, until it would seem that nothing more could be said. To such a degree is this weight of literature felt, that the author of another book almost feels like apologizing for his presumption in writing it. However, the writer of the present volume feels strongly that the ground of Lincoln's life has not yet been fully, correctly or adequately covered, and that the final Lincoln biography is yet to be written.

This little book, of course, makes no attempt to cover any part of Lincoln's life in an exhaustive manner; it merely calls attention to a limited but important phase of his career which has never before been satisfactorily presented. The description of Lincoln's relationship with a particular city is not entirely a new method of procedure: W. E. Barton and B. C. Bryner have already pointed out Lincoln's connection with Chicago and Peoria respectively. However, the relative importance of these cities in the career of Lincoln, as compared to Bloomington, Illinois, is left for the reader to decide after he has finished reading this book.

The writer is aware that much of the material here presented has been previously published, but the sources are so remote, widely scattered, and in some cases so difficult of access, that very few people are acquainted with them. To many this phase of Lincoln's life is practically unknown. The same may be said of the illustrations reproduced, most of which are familiar only to a limited number of local readers. For these reasons the author ventures to submit this addition to Lincoln literature.

I wish to thank Prof. Harry E. Pratt, of Illinois Wesleyan University, Bloomington, Illinois, for his checking of data not available outside of Bloomington.

S. D. W.

New York, N. Y.

HOW

L I N C O L N

Became President

★

I

IT is generally conceded that a man is what his heredity and environment make him. Many extensive researches have been instituted and much has been written of late concerning the heredity of Abraham Lincoln, but comparatively little attention has been given to the environment which chiefly contributed toward fitting him for the Presidency and making him President of the United States. There is not a single "Life of Lincoln," not even any of those by recent writers, which adequately explains how Lincoln became President. Miss Ida M. Tarbell, the late Rev. William E. Barton, Carl Sandburg and the late Hon. Albert J. Beveridge have all had opportunities to obtain the key to the secret of Lincoln's career, and all of them in recent writings have attempted it, but not one of them has completely succeeded. That heredity alone could not have made Lincoln President is shown by Mr. Barton

1

as follows: [1] "Oregon could have made Lincoln a Senator, but it is not certain that any other State than Illinois could have made him President. He needed essentially the conditions which he found in Illinois to develop the qualities which were inherent in him; and he needed a political situation such as existed in Illinois to make him at the opportune time the President of the United States. . . . We can never be quite sure what another State might have done. We are quite certain that no other State, then in the Union, could have furnished all the conditions which Illinois supplied and which were so important both in the evolution of Lincoln and in his elevation." What Mr. Barton says of Illinois in general can be further narrowed down to Bloomington, Illinois, as I propose to show in this book. Lincoln did not become President merely through his own ability. To be sure this was the ultimate cause of his success, but there were other factors in the situation. One of these was that he became fitted for office through hard experience in association with men of unusual capacity; and another, that he won the support of three influential men in Bloomington who devoted themselves with untiring energy to his cause. What the conditions were of Lincoln's preparation, how he became President, and who the men were who "gave him" to the American people and the rest of the world—these are the

[1] Barton, W. E., "The Influence of Illinois in the Development of Abraham Lincoln" in Illinois State Historical Society, *Transactions,* vol. xxviii (Springfield, Ill. 1921) p. 42.

main topics I wish to present at least in outline in the ensuing pages. Since this subject is of the first historical importance, and has never been presented so fully before, I feel it my duty to quote at length when I can introduce first-hand material, and trust that it will not be unwelcome to the reader.

II

WHAT is now an important municipality in Illinois, Bloomington, Seat of McLean County, a residential city of some 35,000 in population today, was founded in the year 1831. Two years later there came to the then small hamlet of about 100 inhabitants, to take up his residence there, a man who was destined to exert a great influence on the surrounding country and the entire nation—Jesse W. Fell.[1] He was born in New Garden Township, Chester county, Pennsylvania, on November 10, 1808, of Quaker parentage. As he had studied law for two years with a firm at Steubenville, Ohio, before he came to Illinois, he opened a law-office at Bloomington in the spring of 1833, establishing himself as the first lawyer of that city. In the fall of 1834 he was introduced to Abraham Lincoln by John T.

[1] Weldon, Lawrence, "Memorial on Jesse W. Fell" in McLean Co. Historical Soc., *Transactions.* 3 vols. (Bloomington 1899-1903) vol. i, p. 338-51.

Morehouse, F. M. I., *The Life of Jesse W. Fell.* University of Ill. Studies in the Social Sciences, vol. v, no. 2 (Urbana 1916).

Stuart at Vandalia, then the State Capital, and there began his long and intimate friendship with the great Emancipator. However, Mr. Fell practiced law only until 1836, when he became so interested in real estate that he turned his office and practice over to David Davis, whom we shall meet shortly. Soon after, on January 14, 1837, he established in cooperation with James Allin, the founder of Bloomington, and Asahel Gridley, one of Bloomington's leading citizens, a weekly newspaper called the *Bloomington Observer,* which was the first newspaper published in Bloomington. In 1857, Mr. Fell became intensely interested in horticulture and the beautifying of his adopted city, and he began to plant trees in Bloomington and North Bloomington (now Normal), which ended only with his death. He planted over 25,000 trees in Normal alone, between twelve and thirteen thousand of them before a house was built there. No wonder that Bloomington is one of the most beautiful cities in Illinois today! Mr. Fell was the founder of Normal, and was largely responsible for the location of the Illinois State Normal University and the Soldiers' Orphans' Home there in later years. Though he was unrivaled as a politician he was never self-seeking, and he generally refused the many offices which were offered to him. What few he did accept were used to accomplish definite ends of service, and he resigned from them as soon as the ends were attained.

While thus introducing Mr. J. W. Fell to the reader, it might be well also to mention one of his younger brothers, Mr. Kersey H. Fell, who plays a minor part in the story to be unfolded. He came to Bloomington in the spring of 1836 and became a clerk in the store of O. Covel and A. Gridley. At one time "he had occasion to go to Springfield in the interest of his employers and while there called at the office of the Hon. J. T. Stuart who was practicing law. Here he met Abraham Lincoln, a young law student. After some conversation with young Abraham, Mr. Fell came to the conclusion that, if Mr. Lincoln could study law with as little education as he had, Mr. Fell would do the same." [1] Accordingly he read law in his leisure hours, and during the winter of 1840-41 he was admitted to the Illinois bar. From 1838 to 1840 Mr. Fell served as clerk with the power to organize DeWitt county, after which he became deputy clerk of the circuit court in Bloomington under Gen. Covel. Thereafter he practiced law in Bloomington for many years, on occasion influencing the course of events as we shall see later.

III

IN 1834, where we find it convenient to begin our narrative, we find Abraham Lincoln living in New Salem, Illinois, acting as a surveyor

[1] Duis, E. *The Good Old Times in McLean County, Illinois* (Bloomington 1874) p. 331-32.

and post master. But twenty-five years of age
he was just beginning to find himself, and with
the help of John T. Stuart had begun the study
of law. Campaigning for the second time in his
life, for a position in the Legislature, he was duly
elected for a term in the Ninth Illinois Assembly.
It was at this time that he made the acquaintance
and friendship of Jesse W. Fell, which was to
mean so much to him in later life. The only event-
ful thing in the life of Lincoln during the years
from 1834 to 1836 was his romance with Ann
Rutledge whose death caused him nameless an-
guish of heart and soul. But he continued his law
studies, and was admitted to the Illinois bar on
March 24, 1836. In the fall of the same year he
was reelected to the Legislature for another two
years, after which he was reelected again. The
following year he moved to Springfield and became the law partner of his friend and mentor,
John T. Stuart, their card appearing for the first
time in the *Sangamon Journal* of April 12, 1837.
This partnership with Stuart was the beginning
of Lincoln's close association and active practice
with the finest lawyers in the United States, without which Lincoln would not have gained the experience which developed his natural talents to
the utmost.

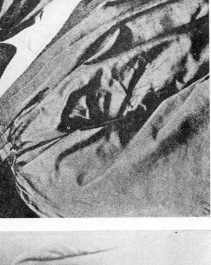

DAVID DAVIS

JESSE W. FELL

IV

A NOTHER character now enters our field of vision in the person of David Davis.[1] He was born at "The Rounds," Sassafras Neck, Cecil Co., Maryland, on March 9, 1815. After graduating from Kenyon College, on September 4, 1832, he studied law for two years with Hon. Henry W. Bishop of Lenox, Mass., and then at the Law School in New Haven, Conn., for a year. In 1835 he moved to Pekin, Ill., and on January 7, 1836 he was admitted to the Illinois Bar. But Davis was about to return to Maryland when Jesse W. Fell induced him to move to Bloomington and offered him his law practice and financial aid. He accepted, took possession of Mr. Fell's office, and became successful at once. It was about this time that Davis first met Abraham Lincoln, but exactly what time and under what circumstances we are not informed. It is safe to say, however, that neither one had any conception how important and far-reaching their friendship was to become. Four years later he was the Whig candidate for the office of State

[1] Swett, Leonard, "The Life and Services of David Davis" in Illinois State Bar Association, *Proceedings,* vol. x (Springfield 1887) p. 75-81.

Weldon, Lawrence, "A Davis Memorial" in McLean Co. Historical Soc., *Op. cit.,* vol. i (1899) p. 320-26.

Dent, Thomas, "David Davis of Illinois—a Sketch" in *American Law Review,* vol. liii (1919) 535-60.

Pratt, H. E., "David Davis, 1815-1886" in Illinois State Historical Soc., *Transactions,* vol. xxxvii (Springfield 1930) p. 157-83.

Senator against Governor Moore, but was defeated. However, in 1844 he was elected Representative from McLean county in the Lower House of the 14th General Assembly of Illinois, declining to be a candidate for reelection. In 1847 Davis was elected a member of the Illinois Constitutional Convention, the second convention of its kind ever held in the State. Here we will leave Davis for a time and return to take up the thread of Lincoln's career.

V

IT is impossible to say definitely when Lincoln made his first trip to Bloomington.   The earliest visit of which we have record probably took place in the summer of 1837, as the following account of it indicates: [1]

Shortly after he became associated with Stuart, the latter sent him to try a case in McLean County for an Englishman named Baddeley, giving him a letter of introduction which advised the client that he could rely upon the bearer to try his case in the best possible manner.

Baddeley inspected his counsel's partner with amazement and chagrin. The young man was six feet four, awkward, ungainly and apparently shy. He was dressed in ill-fitting homespun clothes, the trousers a little too short, and the coat a trifle too large. He had the appearance "of a rustic on his first visit to the circus," and as the client gazed on him, his astonishment turned to indigna-

[1] Hill, F. T., *Lincoln the Lawyer* (New York 1906) p. 80-81.

tion and rage. What did Stuart mean by sending a bumpkin of that sort to represent him? It was preposterous, insulting, and not to be endured.

Without attempting to conceal his disgust Baddeley unceremoniously dispensed with Lincoln's services and straightway retained James A. McDougall, later a United States senator from California, to take charge of the case. History does not relate whether the irate Englishman won or lost the cause, but we know that he lived to become one of Lincoln's most ardent admirers.

About a year later, on May 9, 1838, Lincoln had occasion to go to Bloomington again when he was appointed guardian of the infant heirs of Meril Lyon, deceased, by Judge Jesse B. Thomas.[1] The following September 25th in a chancery bill to foreclose a mortgage, Lincoln is mentioned again in the same connection.[2] Thus Lincoln's association with Bloomington dates almost as early as does his residence in Springfield.

VI

THE importance of the influence of the Eighth Judicial Circuit of Illinois upon the career of Lincoln has generally been suspected, and accordingly nearly every book about him contains some reference to it. But most of them, however authoritative they may appear to be, err upon one or more of three points concerning it, *i. e.,* the

[1] McLean County Circuit Court, *Record,* vol. i, p. 220.
[2] *Ibid,* p. 294.

date of its organization, the number of counties it covered, and the length of time Lincoln traveled on it. Every new writer seems to copy the works of others without verification, and nobody apparently has thought to go to the source material—the laws which established and controlled the circuit. Even as authoritative a book as the third volume of the *Transactions* of the McLean Co. (Ill.) Historical Society states that the Eighth Circuit was organized in 1847 (p. 16); Miss Ida M. Tarbell in her book *In the Footsteps of the Lincolns* (p. 306) includes Coles county in her 1847 map of the Eighth Circuit to total fifteen counties; while on page 303 of the same book Miss Tarbell limits Lincoln's circuit riding between the years 1847 and 1857. In fact, all the tablets now erected along the route of the Eighth Circuit and placed in the Court House Squares of all the County Seats of the Circuit also confine Lincoln's circuit riding within those two dates. Even W. E. Barton's special appendix on the Circuit in his supposedly authoritative book,[1] makes the quadruple error of organizing the Circuit in 1847; saying it remained unchanged for over a decade; making it consist of 13 counties, by leaving out McLean the most important one of all; and confining Lincoln's travel on it to 1847-1859. I shall now present the facts regarding Lincoln and the Eighth Circuit.

[1] *The Life of Abraham Lincoln* 2 vols. (Indianapolis 1925) vol. i, p. 496.

The Eighth Judicial Circuit of Illinois was organized on December 3, 1838, to take effect February 23, 1839, and to include the eight counties of Sangamon, Menard, Tazewell, Livingston, McLean, Logan, Macon and Dane (11 *Session Laws,* p. 155). Stephen T. Logan was commissioned Judge, but he resigned and was succeeded on May 27, 1839 by Samuel H. Treat, who remained Circuit Judge until 1848. On February 1, 1840 the Circuit was reorganized to include the nine counties of Sangamon, Menard, Tazewell, Livingston, McLean, Logan, DeWitt, Macon and Christian (formerly Dane), (11 *Special Session Laws,* p. 5-6). On February 23, 1841 the Circuit was enlarged to include the thirteen counties of Sangamon, Menard, Mason, Tazewell, Livingston, McLean, Logan, DeWitt, Piatt, Champaign, Shelby, Macon and Christian (12 *Session Laws,* p. 108-09). Again, on February 28, 1843, the Circuit was further enlarged to embody the fifteen counties of Sangamon, Menard, Mason, Tazewell, Woodford, Livingston, McLean, Logan, DeWitt, Piatt, Champaign, Shelby, Moultrie, Macon and Christian (13 *Session Laws,* p. 132). On February 21, 1845 the Circuit remained at fifteen counties, but the counties of Mason and Shelby were dropped and the counties of Vermilion and Edgar were put in their place (14 *Session Laws,* p. 48). Fifteen counties at any one time was the greatest extent of the Eighth Circuit. It is clear, then, that the

Circuit had been operating eight years at the time some historians state that it was organized, and that it was made up of a varying number of counties.

Far from Lincoln's circuit riding beginning in 1847, there is every indication that it commenced with the organization of the Circuit in 1839. For instance, we have written in Lincoln's own hand the words: "State of Illinois, Sangamon County and Circuit—of the July term of the Sangamon Circuit Court in the Year of Our Lord One Thousand Eight Hundred and Thirty-Nine."[1] Then, too, we know that the firm of Stuart & Lincoln traveled on the Eighth Circuit,[2] and that firm ended in 1841. Also we have a letter Lincoln wrote to Miss Mary Speed of Louisville, Ky., from Bloomington, and dated September 27, 1841.[3] The Judge's minutes and other indications show that Lincoln traveled the Circuit through 1842 and 1843 even up to his election to Congress in 1846.[4] Again, many of the famous Lincoln stories have clustered about Judge Treat's court as also later about Judge Davis's court. For example, Lincoln's law partner Herndon writes:[5]

[1] Sandburg, Carl, *Abraham Lincoln: The Prairie Years.* 2 vols. (New York 1926) vol. i, p. 221.
[2] Hill, F. T., *Op. cit.,* p. 104.
Binns, H. B., *Abraham Lincoln* (London 1907) p. 68.
[3] Sandburg, Carl, *Op. cit.,* vol. i, p. 263.
[4] Moores, C. W., "Abraham Lincoln Lawyer" in Indiana Historical Soc., *Publications,* vol. vii (Greenfield, Ind. 1918-22) 502.
Hill, F. T. *Op. cit.,* p. 126, 164.
[5] Herndon, W. H. and Weik, J. W., *Herndon's Life of Lincoln,* ed. by P. M. Angle (New York 1930) p. 251.

"I have seen Judge Treat, who was the very impersonation of gravity itself, sit up till the last and laugh until, as he often expressed it, 'he almost shook his ribs loose.'" Again contrary to the statement of most biographers, Lincoln did not end his circuit riding in 1857, but continued it to the time of his nomination for the presidency —the spring of 1860.[1] Thus the period of Lincoln's circuit riding should be changed on the County Seat markers, at least in Bloomington and Lincoln, Illinois, from 1847-1857 to 1839-1860.

VII

NOW to catch up with our story. At the expiration of his term in the Legislature in 1840 Lincoln was again reelected to that office. On April 14, 1841 he parted company with John T. Stuart and formed a law partnership with Judge Stephen T. Logan, which gave him further practice with the best lawyers in the country. On November 4, 1842 he was married to Mary Todd who, it is said, was ambitious for social position and saw in the uncouth Lincoln at this early date great promise of what was to follow. On September 20, 1843 Lincoln dissolved his partnership with Judge Logan and became the partner of

[1] McLean Co. Historical Soc., *Op. cit.*, vol. iii (1900) p. 18.
Lamon, W. H., *The Life of Abraham Lincoln* (Boston 1872) p. 323.
Hill, F. T. *Op. cit.*, p. 169.

William H. Herndon, a connection which lasted until Lincoln's death in 1865—long after he had become President and no longer lived in Springfield. In the latter part of the year 1846 Lincoln was elected to Congress on the Whig ticket over his rival, the Rev. Peter Cartwright, and his departure for Washington in November of the following year concludes a definite period in his career and in our narrative. He was a representative in Congress for the Seventh Illinois district, of which McLean county was a part.

VIII

WE now begin the exposition of the period in the life of Lincoln, extending primarily to his nomination for the Presidency, which is the object of this book. On February 11, 1847 the Eighth Judicial Circuit was reorganized to contain the fourteen counties of Sangamon, Tazewell, Woodford, McLean, Logan, DeWitt, Piatt, Champaign, Vermilion, Edgar, Shelby, Moultrie, Macon and Christian (15 *Session Laws,* p. 31). The Circuit made up in this way, lasting until 1853, was its form when made famous by Lincoln. Judge Samuel H. Treat was its presiding Justice until early in September, 1848, when David Davis of Bloomington was elected to fill the place. The figure of Judge Davis is second only to Abraham Lincoln in those

romantic qualities which have made the Eighth
Circuit famous. The dimensions of the Eighth
Circuit during this period were at least 110 x 140
miles, and the journey to the fourteen county
seats was about 500 miles in length. Today there
are eighteen Judges in the same district covered
by one Justice in those early days.

IX

AN early glimpse of Lincoln in Bloomington,
during the first term of court under Judge
Davis, in September, 1848, is given to us by Ward
Hill Lamon.[1] Mr. Lamon later became Lincoln's
local law partner in Danville and after 1858 in
Bloomington, and finally was appointed by Lin-
coln the Marshal of the District of Columbia.
Mr. Lamon's amusing story now follows:

The following incident, which illustrates his [Lin-
coln's] love of a joke, occurred in the early days of our
acquaintance. I, being at the time on the infant side of
twenty-one, took particular pleasure in athletic sports.
One day when we were attending the circuit court which
met at Bloomington, Ill., I was wrestling near the court
house with some one who had challenged me to a trial,
and in the scuffle made a large rent in the rear of my
trousers. Before I had time to make any change, I was

[1] Lamon, W. H., *Recollections of Abraham Lincoln, 1847-1865,*
ed. by D. L. Teillard (2nd ed. Washington 1911) p. 16-17. For their
relations in general, see Tilton, C. C., "Lincoln and Lamon: Partners and Friends" in Illinois State Historical Soc., *Transactions,*
vol. xxxviii (1931) p. 175-228.

called into court to take up a case. The evidence was finished. I, being the Prosecuting Attorney at the time, got up to address the jury. Having on a somewhat short coat, my misfortune was rather apparent. One of the lawyers for a joke, started a subscription paper which was passed from one member of the bar to another as they sat by a long table fronting the bench, to buy a pair of pantaloons for Lamon,—"he being," the paper said, "a poor but worthy young man." Several put down their names with some ludicrous subscription, and finally the paper was laid by some one in front of Mr. Lincoln, he being engaged in writing at the time. He quietly glanced over the paper, and immediately taking up his pen, wrote after his name, "I can contribute nothing to the end in view."

X

THE third main character in our narrative now appears—Leonard Swett.[1] He was born near the village of Turner, Oxford Co., Maine, on August 11, 1825. Having studied three years at Waterville College—now Colby University—at the age of twenty, he read law for two years with the firm of Howard & Shepley, at Portland, Maine, and then set out to make his way in the world. He traveled for nearly a year in the South, and finally volunteered to serve in the Mexican War under General Winfield Scott. During his service he contracted a disease from which he nearly died, and while in a weakened

[1] Swett, L. H., "Leonard Swett" in McLean Co. Historical Soc., *Op. Cit.,* vol. ii (1903) p. 332-65.

condition he was sent on his way home after having been discharged from Jefferson Barracks, near St. Louis. But his strength gave out when he reached Peoria, Illinois, from which city in the month of July, 1848, he found his way to Bloomington. There he settled down, spending the first year in regaining his health, teaching school and reading law. In June, 1849, he was admitted to the bar, and began the active practice of law. He has described in the following words the memorable occasion of his first meeting with Abraham Lincoln:[2]

In the autumn of 1849, I was sitting with Judge David Davis in a small country hotel in Mt. Pulaski, Illinois, when a tall man, with a circular blue cloak thrown over his shoulders, entered one door of the room, and passing through without speaking, went out another. I was struck by his appearance. It was the first time I had ever seen him, and I said to Judge Davis, when he had gone, "Who is that?" "Why, don't you know him? That is Lincoln." In a few moments he returned, and, for the first time, I shook the hand and made the acquaintance of that man who since then has so wonderfully impressed himself upon the hearts and affections of mankind. . . . Mr. Lincoln had, just before that time, closed his only term in Congress, and had, when I met him, returned to his former life as a lawyer upon this, the Eighth Judicial Circuit.

The friendship of Swett with Lincoln, like those of Fell and Davis with Lincoln, was to have

[2] Rice, A. T., ed., *Reminiscences of Abraham Lincoln by Distinguished Men of his Time* (New York 1886) p. 455-56.

far-reaching significance for the future history of the country.

XI

ONE more character requires brief mention, since he takes a comparatively minor part in our story. Reference is made to him only because he was a friend of Lincoln, one of his Bloomington "boosters," and because he explains the author's basic interest and knowledge in the subject matter herein set forth. Dr. Cyrenius Wakefield,[1] grandfather of the writer, was born in 1815 at Watertown, N. Y., but migrated to a farm near Bloomington in the year 1837. In September, 1849, he purchased two lots and a two-story frame house on the south side of the Court-House Square in Bloomington, beside which he built a three-story building which was known as "Wakefield's New Brick." Here he established a drug store, followed in 1851 by a weekly newspaper known as the *Illinois State Bulletin*. Dr. Wakefield now made Bloomington his permanent home, and built in 1852 a residence on East Washington street. It was in this residence that he often entertained Lincoln when the latter was in town.

[1] Duis, E., *Op. cit.*, p. 354-58.
Burnham, J. H. in *The History of McLean County, Illinois* (Chicago 1879) p. 826-27.
Wakefield, Homer, *Wakefield Memorial* (Bloomington 1897) p. 82-86.
Hasbrouck, J. L., *History of McLean County, Illinois.* 2 vols. (Topeka 1924) vol i, p. 408-10.

DR. CYRENIUS WAKEFIELD

LEONARD SWETT

XII

IN March, 1849, Lincoln returned to Illinois
from his term in Congress, and took up with
renewed vigor his former life on the Eighth Judicial Circuit, now under the leadership of Judge
David Davis of Bloomington. Mr. Frederick
T. Hill tells us that "Lincoln did not return to
any assured clientage at the close of his congressional term, and he had his professional reputation still to make when he began to follow Judge
Davis over the circuit." [1] Lincoln spent over half
of every year riding the circuit. The lawyers arrived at a county seat of from five hundred to two
thousand inhabitants, and the clients and public
came from the country adjoining at the same
time. The lawyers were then employed in such
suits as would be pending in court, and the trials
began immediately. After from three days to two
weeks spent in this manner, the court adjourned
and moved on to the next county seat, where the
same process was repeated. Davis and Lincoln
were the only lawyers who traveled the whole circuit—Davis because he was obliged to and Lincoln because he loved it. Beginning in 1849 Leonard Swett covered part of the circuit with them,
and after 1857 he traveled the entire reduced circuit of five counties.[2] But life on the circuit was

---

[1] Hill, F. T., *Op. cit.*, p. 196.
[2] Leonard Swett in Oldroyd, O. H., *Lincoln's Campaign* (Chicago 1896) p. 70.
   Mrs. Jane Martin Johns of Decatur in Barton, W. E., *The Soul
of Abraham Lincoln* (New York 1920) p. 249.

not easy. Leonard Swett some years later said: [1]
"I rode the Eighth Judicial Circuit with Lincoln
for eleven years, and in the allotment between
him and the large Judge Davis in the scanty provision of these times, as a rule I slept with him.
Beds were always too short, coffee in the morning
burned or otherwise bad, food often indifferent,
roads simply trails, streams without bridges and
often swollen, and had to be swam, sloughs often
muddy and almost impassable, and we had to
help the horses when the wagon mired down, with
fence rails for pries." A typical story of the hard-
ships involved is told as follows: [2]

At one time Judge Davis and Abraham Lincoln were
traveling on horseback to attend court at Decatur.
When they reached the Sangamon River it was late at
night, and it was necessary for them to be in Decatur on
the following morning. But as they could see nothing
ahead of them, Lincoln gave up the idea of proceeding
further. When they came to the river's bank Judge
Davis, without saying a word, plunged into the stream
with his horse and swam across; but being unable in the
darkness to find a landing, returned to the point from
which he started. After going some distance down stream
Judge Davis again swam across and this time was fortunate enough to find a landing. Then with the assistance of some farmers he built a fire on the bank of the
river to show Mr. Lincoln where to land, if he chose to
swim over. The latter swam towards the light and was
safely landed, and on the following morning both parties
were enabled to be in attendance at court.

[1] Moores, C. W., *Op. cit.*, p. 503-04.
[2] Duis, E., *Op. cit.*, p. 287-88.

Hard though it was, the influence of the Eighth Circuit upon the career of Lincoln can scarcely be overestimated—there, for the most part, were the conditions which made him President of the United States. First of all were the talented lawyers with whom he associated—such men as John T. Stuart; Judge Stephen T. Logan, whom Judge Davis called the ablest lawyer he had ever met; Judge Samuel H. Treat, later Chief Justice of the State of Illinois; Judge David Davis, later Associate Justice of the Supreme Court of the United States; Judge Stephen A. Douglas, and others. It was also on the Circuit that Lincoln made the friendship of all sorts of people, and where he first became famous. But it was principally his friends in Bloomington, headed by Jesse W. Fell, Judge David Davis and Leonard Swett, who created his country-wide fame, conceived of him as President, and secured his nomination.

XIII

ON two widely separated pages in his biography of Lincoln, Herndon[1] states that Lincoln never took advantage of the many land values to be obtained in the Middle West. Beveridge[2] is nearer the truth when he says: "With

[1] Herndon, W. H., *Op. cit.*, p. 99, 279.
[2] Beveridge, A. J., *Abraham Lincoln, 1809-1858.* 2 vols. (Boston 1928) vol. i, p. 553.

the exception of his lot in Springfield and a lot
in Lincoln, the county seat of Logan County, the
Iowa farm is the only real estate he ever owned."
Aside from the fact that Lincoln owned several
lots in Springfield, no mention is made in any biography that he owned two lots in Bloomington.[3]
In October, 1851, Lincoln bought two lots on the
corner of Jefferson and McLean streets, in
Bloomington, for the sum of $325.08. It is pos-
sible that he intended to build a house and live in
Bloomington, as his best friends were there and
he felt more at home than in Springfield. On the
other hand, in spite of Herndon's specific statement to the contrary, he may have purchased
them purely for speculative purposes. The sale
was made through David Davis, as the following
bill of sale (published for the first time) shows:[4]

THIS INDENTURE made this Sixth day of October in
the year of our Lord One Thousand Eight Hundred
Fifty one between Levi Davis and Lucy Ann Davis, wife
of the said Levi, of the City of Alton in the County of
Madison and State of Illinois of the first part and Abraham Lincoln of the City of Springfield in the County
of Sangamon and State of Illinois of the second part,
WITNESSETH: that the said parties of the first part for
and in consideration of the sum of Three Hundred
Twenty-five Dollars and Eight Cents, in hand paid by

[3] "Lincoln's Bloomington Lots" in Abraham Lincoln Association,
Bulletin, no. xvii (Springfield, Ill. 1929) p. 4. The price of purchase given is wrong. Bloomington *Daily Pantagraph,* Aug. 26,
1930. p. 5B. The price of sale given is incorrect.
[4] McLean Co. Court, *Deeds,* Book ii, p. 174. Filed Oct. 11, 1851.
Recorded Oct. 29, 1851.

the said party of the second part, the receipt whereof is hereby acknowledged, have granted, bargained, sold, remised, released, aliened and confirmed and by these presents do grant, bargain, sell, remise, release, alien and confirm unto the said party of the second part and to his heirs and assigns forever all those lots or parcels of land known and described as follows, to-wit:

Lots Eleven and Twelve in Block Two in Evan's Addition to the late Town, now City of Bloomington, in the County of McLean and State of Illinois aforesaid, together with all and singular the hereditaments and appurtenances thereunto belonging or in any wise appertaining and all the estate, right, title and interest, of the said parties of the first part either in law or equity of, in and to the above bargained premises; to have and to hold said premises as above described with the appurtenances unto the said party of the second part and to his heirs and assigns forever and the said Levi Davis for himself and for his heirs, executors and administrators, does covenant, grant, bargain and agree to and with the said party of the second part and his heirs and assigns that at the time of the ensealing and delivery of these presents he is well seized of the premises above conveyed as in fee simple and has good right, full power and lawful authority to grant, bargain, sell and convey the same in manner and form as aforesaid and that the same are free and clear of all encumbrances of every kind and nature soever. And the above bargained premises in the quiet and peaceable possession of the said party of the second part, his heirs and assigns, against all and every person or persons lawfully claiming or to claim the whole or any part thereof, he will forever warrant and defend.

In testimony whereof the said parties of the first part have hereunto set their hands the day and year first above written.

Signed, sealed and delivered   LEVI DAVIS   (*Seal*)
   in the presence of   LUCY ANN DAVIS (*Seal*)
    JOHN F. STUWART   BY DAVID DAVIS   (*Seal*)
                       Their Attorney-in-fact

STATE OF ILLINOIS)
) ss.
LOGAN COUNTY   )

Before me, the undersigned Clerk of the Circuit Court in and for the County and State aforesaid personally appeared David Davis, who is personally known to me to be the real person whose name is subscribed to the foregoing and as having executed the same as attorney-in-fact for said Levi Davis and Lucy Ann Davis, and acknowledged the same to be his act and deed for the purposes therein expressed.

Given under my hand and seal of office this Sixth day of October in the year of our Lord One Thousand Eight Hundred Fifty-one.

                      SAMUEL EMMETT
                           Clerk

XIV

THE chief political event in the year 1852 was the Presidential campaign between Brigadier-General Franklin Pierce, the Democratic candidate, and General Winfield Scott, late hero of the Mexican War, the Whig candidate. Although an important year, little is known of Lincoln's activities at that time, and in his published *Works* that year is a blank. It is known that Lincoln made two addresses before the Scott Club in Springfield during August on behalf of General

Scott and against a previous address by Stephen A. Douglas for General Pierce. The Hon. Adlai E. Stevenson, Vice-President of the United States in 1893-97, and for many years a resident of Bloomington, has left us the following early glimpse of Lincoln in Bloomington and record of another address by him for General Scott: [1]

I distinctly recall the first time I saw Mr. Lincoln. In September, 1852, two lawyers from Springfield, somewhat travel-stained with their sixty miles' journey, alighted from the stage-coach in front of the old tavern in Bloomington. The taller and younger of the two was Abraham Lincoln; the other, his personal friend and former preceptor, John T. Stuart. That evening it was my good fortune to hear Mr. Lincoln address a political meeting at the old Courthouse in advocacy of the election of General Winfield Scott to the Presidency. The speech was one of great ability, and but little that was favorable of the military record of General Pierce remained when the speech was concluded. The Mexican War was then of recent occurrence, its startling events fresh in the memory of all, and its heroes still the heroes of the hour. The more than half-century that has passed has not wholly dispelled my recollection of Mr. Lincoln's eloquent tribute to "the hero of Lundy's Lane," and his humorous description of the military career of General Franklin Pierce.

But on election day every state in the union, except four, including Illinois, voted for General Pierce.

[1] Stevenson, A. E., *Something of Men I Have Known* (Chicago 1909) p. 8.

XV

THERE is a well-known letter written by Abraham Lincoln to Mr. Richard Price Morgan, on February 13, 1856, when the latter became Superintendent of the Chicago and Alton Railroad, asking in characteristic vein for a renewal of his pass on that road. Mr. Morgan, who later founded the town of Dwight, Ill., gives us an interesting vignette of Lincoln in Bloomington during September, 1853: [2]

I had the good fortune to become acquainted with him [Mr. Lincoln] in Bloomington in 1853, when I was division engineer, building the Chicago & Alton Railroad. Bloomington was then a village of 1,200 people, overcrowded with emigrants, land buyers, railway contractors and laborers. Being somewhat permanently located, I was fortunate enough to have a large room on the first floor of my boarding-house, to which circumstance I am indebted for my acquaintance with Mr. Lincoln. On a hot afternoon, I think in the autumn season, I was seated in my room with the door partly open to the main hall, when I overheard the following conversation: "Indeed, if you cannot accommodate me, I am sure I do not know what I shall do. I am here for this term of the Circuit Court, and have tried everywhere to find accommodations, but so far have failed, and I see no probability of success unless you can care for me." The landlady, to whom the above was addressed, replied:

[2] Morgan, R. P. in Phillips, I. N., ed., *Abraham Lincoln by Some Men Who Knew Him* (Bloomington 1910) p. 95-100.

"Mr. Lincoln, I would like very much to give you a room and board while you are in the city, but I have no room or bed to offer you; but if it will help you any to come here for your meals, I will do the best I can for you." "Well," said Mr. Lincoln, "you are very kind, but I have nowhere to lay my head."

Those being early days of western life, of which I had seen something, I stepped to the hall door and for the first time saw the tall man of destiny. After a moment, I said to the landlady: "Is this gentleman a friend of yours?" To which she replied, introducing him as 'Mr. Lincoln, of Springfield, a lawyer who is practicing in the court of McLean county.' He is a friend of mine, and I am very sorry indeed that I am unable to accommodate him." After looking at Mr. Lincoln a moment, and he at me, with a rather inquiring expression, I said: "If you will put a bed in my room, which is too large for one person in these crowded times, I would be pleased to have Mr. Lincoln room with me during his stay in the city." As I finished this remark, Lincoln threw back his head a little, and with it the long black hair that came over his forehead, and said: "Now, that is what I call clever." (In common western parlance the word "clever" was often used in the sense of kind or accommodating).

I thus became the roommate of the greatest man since Washington, the peer of any man in the love of liberty, justice and mercy; and I wish to record here that during the time of this stay—several [two?] weeks—I learned from him many things which have been of priceless value to me.

Although his time was very much engrossed by court proceedings, he seemed to strive, although I was twenty years his junior, to make his companionship interesting and serviceable to me. I was told by him of many things and stories of the earlier settlers in Illinois, and also he recited selections of poetry, one of them being the poem, "Oh, why should the spirit of mortal be proud?" of which he was very fond.

One evening he said: "The people of McLean county, before they became interested in railway construction, and when Pekin, on the Illinois River, was their market, had very little to occupy their time, especially at some seasons of the year. They would come to Bloomington on Saturdays with all sorts of vehicles—wagons, carts, and on horseback—and put in most of the day in fun, horse racing, settling old feuds, etc. When evening came and they were about to separate and return to their homes, almost every man, besides being well filled before starting, carried with him a good-sized brown jug in the front end of his wagon or cart."

Speaking of the relative merits of New England rum and corn juice, as he called it, to illuminate the human mind, he told me this story of John Moore, who resided south of Blooming Grove, and subsequently became State Treasurer: Mr. Moore came to Bloomington one Saturday in a cart drawn by a fine pair of young red steers. For some reason he was a little late starting home, and besides his brown jug, he otherwise had a good load on. In passing through the grove that night, one wheel of his cart struck a stump or root and threw the pole out of the ring of the yoke. The steers, finding themselves free, ran away, and left John Moore sound asleep in his cart, where he remained all night. Early in the morning he roused himself, and looking over the side of the cart and around in the woods, he said: "If my name is John Moore, I've lost a pair of steers; if my name ain't John Moore, I've found a cart." After a good laugh together, Lincoln said: "Morgan, if you ever tell this story, you must add that Moore told it on himself."

XVI

IN the fall of 1853 Abraham Lincoln started what turned out to be the most lucrative lawsuit of his career. On February 3rd of that year, due to the increase in population of the State, the Eighth Circuit had been reduced to the eight counties of Sangamon, Tazewell, Woodford, McLean, Logan, DeWitt, Champaign and Vermilion (18 *Session Laws,* p. 63). The following letter,[1] written by Lincoln to Thompson R. Webber, Clerk of the Court of Champaign County, introduces us to Lincoln's most important law case:

BLOOMINGTON, *Sept. 12, 1853.*

T. R. WEBBER, ESQ.
My dear Sir:

On my arrival here to court, I find that McLean county has assessed the land and other property of the Central Railroad for the purpose of county taxation. An effort is about to be made to get the question of the right to so tax the Co. before the court and ultimately before the supreme court, and the Co. are offering to engage me for them. As this will be the same question I have had under consideration for you, I am somewhat trammelled by what has passed between you and me, feeling that you have the first right to my services, if you choose to secure me a fee something near such as I can get from the other side.

The question in its magnitude to the Co. on the one

[1] Lincoln, Abraham, *Uncollected Letters of Abraham Lincoln,* ed. by G. A. Tracy (Boston 1917) p. 47.

hand and the counties in which the Co. has land on the other is the largest law question that can now be got up in the State, and therefore in justice to myself, I can not afford, if I can help it, to miss a fee altogether. If you choose to release me, say so by return mail, and there an end. If you wish to retain me, you better get authority from your court, come directly over in the stage and make common cause with this county.

Very truly your friend,

A. Lincoln.

Mr. Webber at once wrote Mr. John B. Thomas, Judge of Champaign County, for advice and authority to act, and in a few days received the following letter: [1]

At Home [Urbana], *Sept. 15, 1853.*

Mr. T. R. Webber,
Dear Sir:—

I did not get home until late last night and in order to communicate with you certainly this morning I send my little boy up with a line. I fully concur with your opinion that no time is to be lost in securing the services of Mr. Lincoln and hope you or Mr. Jaquith [Jesse W. Jaquith, Champaign Co. Associate Judge] will leave immediately for Bloomington, confer with the authorities of McLean and take such measures as the circumstances may suggest as to the fee to be offered Mr. Lincoln. I have only this to say that we have no right to expect his services for a trifle and in this respect have no hesitation in giving you full authority to contract for a fee in proportion to the importance of the claim. I would however suggest that you draw from the Treasury the sum of fifty dollars and take it with you as a retaining

[1] Starr, J. W., *Lincoln and the Railroads* (New York 1927) p. 60-61.

fee (you need not give it all if less will do) and contract for an additional contingent fee such as may be necessary even to $500. I would further recommend if Mr. Jaquith agrees that an order be entered on the record of the County Court authorizing you to make contract with Mr. Lincoln or any other lawyer that may be necessary to carry out the object in view. . . .

I do not know but we had best get the assistance of some other able counsel as well as Mr. Lincoln. Say Judge Breese, Archibald Williams, Logan or J. T. Stuart. . . .

Yours as ever,
JOHN B. THOMAS.

What talks Mr. Webber had with Lincoln we do not know, but less than three weeks later the situation developed with this letter: [1]

PEKIN, *October 3, 1853.*

M. BRAYMAN, ESQ.
Dear Sir:

Neither the county of McLean nor any one on its behalf has yet made any engagement with me in relation to its suit with the Illinois Central Railroad on the subject of taxation. I am now free to make an engagement for the road, and if you think of it you may "count me in." Please write me on receipt of this. I shall be here at least ten days.

Yours truly,
A. LINCOLN.

Mr. Mason Brayman was an attorney for the Illinois Central Railroad. Four days later Lincoln was engaged and a retainer fee of two hun-

[1] Lincoln, Abraham, *Complete Works*, ed. by J. G. Nicolay and John Hay. 12 vols (new ed. New York 1905) vol. ii, p. 179-80.

dred dollars was sent to him. The case was heard
in the Bloomington Circuit Court by Judge
David Davis, and McLean County was victor.
The Railroad, however, appealed to the Supreme
Court of Illinois, and after two hearings the verdict of the lower court was reversed at the December term, 1855.[1] Some of the biographers of
Lincoln in describing this case have made flagrant
errors, which need correcting. The most noto-
rious, and probably the source of the others, were
penned by W. H. Herndon, law-partner of Lincoln, who should have known better. Mr. Herndon states that McLean County started the suit
—that the Railroad was the defendant—that the
Railroad won in the Circuit Court—and that the
County appealed to the Supreme Court.[2] In
every case the official documents prove the contrary. Also Mr. Herndon states that the retainer
fee was $250 instead of $200.[3] In this suit Lincoln was opposed by both his former law partners: John T. Stuart and Judge Stephen T.
Logan.

The settlement of the above case gave rise to

[1] 17 *Illinois*, p. 291-97.

[2] Herndon, W. H., *Op. cit.*, p. 284.

[3] Hon. Albert J. Beveridge in his *Abraham Lincoln, 1809-1858*,
vol. i, p. 587) insists that the retainer fee was $250, but on p. 591
he quotes James S. Ewing and on p. 592 Charles L. Capen, both of
Bloomington, to the effect that the fee was $200. Also on p. 592 and
in vol. ii, p. 522 he states that the amount the Company finally paid
Lincoln was $4,800, which, if the retainer fee was $250, should
have been $4,750. Final proof that the amount was $200 is furnished by the Court records in Bloomington and by the Court notice
in the Bloomington *Daily Pantagraph* for June 24, 1857.

another one even more famous. Some time in December, 1855, Lincoln presented his bill to the Illinois Central Railroad Company for $5,000 in payment of his services. He did not consider this too much for the service rendered, which involved a hearing in the Circuit Court and two before the Supreme Court. Also the importance of the case, which saved the Railroad millions of dollars and settled the general question of railroad taxation for all time, was taken into consideration. But the general counsel for the Road refused to pay the amount, saying it was as much as a first-class lawyer like Daniel Webster would have charged. "I think," related Mr. James F. Joy, who was one of the Railroad's counsel, some time later, "there would have been no difficulty with Mr. Lincoln's bill if I had charged as, perhaps, I ought to have done, five thousand dollars. The time for such fees as the lawyers now ask had not arrived, and my own charge for the arguments in the case was only twelve hundred dollars. I think now my charge was a small one for the service rendered. The railroad company, after declining to pay Mr. Lincoln the five thousand dollars he demanded because it thought the fee was too large, then made him this proposition: 'Bring suit against the company for the amount demanded and no attempt will be made to defend against it. If by the testimony of other lawyers it shall appear to be a fair charge and there shall be a judgment for the amount, then we shall be justified in paying it.' " [1] Stung by his rebuff, Lincoln went to Bloomington and presented the matter to his lawyer friends. They advised him to sue the Railroad for the $5,000 and drew up the following document in his behalf: [2]

THE ILLINOIS CENTRAL RAILROAD COMPANY
To A. LINCOLN DR.

To professional services in the case of the Illinois Central Railroad Company against the County of McLean, argued in the Supreme Court of the State of Illinois at December Term 1855....................$5000.00

We, the undersigned members of the Illinois Bar, understanding that the above entitled cause was twice argued in the Supreme Court, and that the judgment therein decided the question of the claim of counties and other minor municipal corporations to tax the property of said railroad company, and settled said question against said claim and in favor of said railroad company, are of opinion the sum above charged as a fee is not unreasonable.

GRANT GOODRICH	N. H. PURPLE
N. B. JUDD	O. H. BROWNING
ARCHIBALD WILLIAMS	R. S. BLACKWELL

To illustrate the caliber of Lincoln's friends on the Eighth Circuit, of the above six men one later became a Congressman and an ambassador to a European court; one a United States District Judge in a Western State; another a United States Senator and a member of the President's Cabinet at Washington; and the others were

[1] Weik, J. W., *The Real Lincoln* (Boston 1922) p. 153.
[2] Lincoln, Abraham, *Complete Works,* vol. ii, p. 288-89. Herndon, W. H., *Op cit.,* p. 284.

among the ablest and most successful lawyers of
the Illinois bar. During the months of March and
July, 1857, Lincoln found it necessary to make
the tedious and expensive trip to New York in
order to consult with the directors of the Illinois
Central Railroad about his fee, but to no avail.[3]
The case was heard in the Bloomington Circuit
Court by Judge Davis and a jury on the morning
of June 18, 1857. As nobody appeared in behalf
of the Railroad, the jury returned a verdict without leaving their seats for $5,000 for Mr. Lin-
coln. That afternoon, however, Mr. John M.
Douglas of Chicago appeared for the Company
and demanded a new trial. As Lincoln did not
object the case went to the jury a second time, on
June 23rd, and the verdict was again in Lincoln's
favor. But this time he remembered that he had
received a retainer fee of $200 from the Railroad,
and so the judgment was reduced to $4,800—the
largest fee he ever received. The Company paid
the costs of $26.40 and the case was dismissed.
The Railroad Company apparently tried to avoid
paying the fee, for written on the margin of the
Judgment in the McLean Circuit Clerk's office
in Bloomington is found written: "Execution issued to Sheriff Moore, Aug. 1, 1857." On this
threat to seize the property of the Railroad if the
fee was not paid, Lincoln received a check on
August 12, 1857 and deposited it to his account
with the Springfield Fire & Marine Insurance

[3] Beveridge, A. J., *Op cit.,* vol. i, p. 590; vol. ii, p. 520.

Company.[1] These and other facts dispute the later claims of the Railroad that this suit of Lincoln's was amicable and purely a legal technicality. On August 31st Lincoln withdrew from the bank the entire amount of $4,800, and gave half to his partner Herndon, who said, "much as we deprecated the avarice of great corporations, we both thanked the Lord for letting the Illinois Central Railroad fall into our hands."[2]

XVII

THE year 1854, from the very beginning, turned out to be very exciting. On the 4th of January, Senator Stephen A. Douglas reported, as Chairman of the Committee on Territories, a bill to organize the Territory of Nebraska which would embrace all the country west of the State of Missouri and north of a line running through the southern boundary of that State. The bill further provided that when this territory should be divided into states the people residing therein should decide whether or not they desired to have slavery. On the 23rd of the same month a new bill was introduced by Douglas with an amendment proposed by Senator Archibald Dixon of Kentucky which divided the

[1] Townsend, W. H., *Lincoln the Litigant* (Boston 1925) p. 29.
[2] Beveridge, A. J., *Op. cit.*, vol. i, p. 592.
Herndon, W. H., *Op. cit.*, p. 284.

territory into two parts, Kansas and Nebraska, and repealed the Missouri Compromise of 1820. This Kansas-Nebraska Bill became a law of the land on May 30, 1854, and its passage had tremendous consequences. The Missouri Compromise was an agreement between the north and the south by which Missouri was admitted to the Union as a slave-holding state on condition that slavery should be forever prohibited in the territory west and north of that State. The enemies of slavery had come to regard the Missouri Compromise as sacred and inviolate, but now it was repealed and the way was open for the introduction of slavery into the new territory. Great excitement was generated throughout the country, and many meetings were held by abolitionist sympathizers. There was a tendency to form a new political party which had for its main plank opposition to the new law, and which was variously known as Anti-Nebraska or Republican.

XVIII

ONE of the greatest principles in political history came to Lincoln while he was spending the night of January 23, 1854, at the Pike House, the leading hotel of Bloomington. Mr. Frederick T. Hill describes the occasion as follows:[1]

[1] Hill, F. T., *Op. cit.,* p. 264.

Lincoln was attending court on the circuit when this news [of the amendment to the Nebraska Bill] reached him, and Judge Dickey, one of his fellow-practitioners, who was sharing his room in the local tavern at the time, reports that Lincoln sat on the edge of his bed and discussed the political situation far into the night. At last Dickey fell asleep, but when he awoke in the morning, Lincoln was sitting up in bed, deeply absorbed in thought. "I tell you, Dickey," he observed, as though continuing the argument of the previous evening, "this nation cannot exist half-slave and half-free."

Mr. T. Lyle Dickey, not appreciating the importance of Lincoln's conclusion, fretfully replied: "Oh, Lincoln, go to sleep." [1] The principle in question was that set forth by Lincoln on June 17, 1858, in his famous "House Divided" speech, which had a profound effect on future events. He said: " 'A house divided against itself cannot stand.' I believe this government cannot endure; permanently half *slave* and half *free*. I do not expect the Union to be *dissolved*—I do not expect the house to *fall*—but I *do* expect it will cease to be divided. It will become *all* one thing, or *all* the other." [2]

[1] Sandburg, Carl, *Op cit.,* p. 24, 167. Bloomington (Ill.) *Pantagraph,* Feb. 12, 1927. Lincoln was not attending court, as court was not in session then.

[2] Italics Lincoln's. Beveridge, A. J., *Op. cit.,* vol. ii, p. 577.

XIX

O NE of the earliest local meetings calling itself "Republican" which was held in Illinois
was called by the following notice in the Bloomington *Weekly Pantagraph* of Wednesday, September 6, 1854:

A meeting of the citizens of McLean county, favorable
to the organization of a Republic Party, whose platform
shall be Anti-Nebraska and Anti-Liquor traffic, will be
held at the Court House in Bloomington, on Saturday
next at 2 o'clock P. M., for the purpose of appointing
Delegates to the State and District Conventions to be
held here on the 12th and 13th inst.

MANY CITIZENS.

At this meeting, on September 9th, six men
were elected delegates to the State Convention at
Springfield to be held on October 4th and 5th. On
September 12th and 13th the "Republican" Convention of the third Congressional District, referred to above, was held at Major's Hall in
Bloomington. Among the delegates to this Congressional Convention, who came from ten counties, were some known as "Republicans," or Abolitionists, and others were "Anti-Nebraska"
Whigs and Democrats. In the organization of
the Convention the "Republican" element obtained control, and caused to be adopted a full
set of "Republican" resolutions which were intended to displease the Whigs and be too radical

for Jesse O. Norton, of Joliet, who was the Anti-Nebraska and also Old-Line Whig candidate for nomination to Congress. But Norton surprised the Convention by accepting the "Republican" platform. The supporters of the opposing candidate, Mr. C. Coffin, who was also a Whig, then withdrew from Major's Hall and met at the Pike House for their independent deliberations. But Committees conferred between the two wings of the Convention, and at 11 P.M. the seceders returned to Major's Hall and participated in the nomination of Mr. Norton as a "Republican." The following November the Whigs voted for Mr. Norton as a Whig, the "Republicans" as a "Republican," and he was elected to Congress.[1] This Congressional Convention was one of the first efforts in the State of Illinois to form a Republican Party, but it is clear that the attempt was unsuccessful as the elements which should have merged continued to maintain their independent identities. The use of the name "Republican" should not be misleading, as the name is much older than the Party which now bears the name.

XX

SIMULTANEOUSLY with the Congressional Convention on the same two days there was also held in Bloomington a German Anti-

[1] Burnham, J. H., *History of Bloomington and Normal, in McLean County, Illinois* (Bloomington 1879) p. 110-11.

Nebraska State Convention at the Court House.
Abraham Lincoln was in town at the time attending the court sessions, and by request he addressed
the delegates on the evening of the 12th. The
Bloomington *Pantagraph* reported the speech in
part as follows: [1]

We had the satisfaction of listening to an address by
Hon. A. Lincoln, on the subject that is engaging the
attention of the free men of the Union more than any
political question that has been agitated for sometime,
viz: The Nebraska Bill. The speech was clear and unanswerable, for it was a plain statement of facts, and of
sound, strong argument; it was eloquent, for he spoke
the deep convictions of truth from a heart warmed with
the love of his country, and the love of freedom. The
address was not only instructive, and his argument
against the Nebraska outrage unanswerable, but it was
spiced with remarks that were diverting, and at the same
time gave a deeper felt conviction of the weight of sober
argument, for the speaker was Hon. A. Lincoln.

The speech was judiciously timed and admirably calculated to do good, by portraying the nature, and de-
veloping the design of the Nebraska Bill, without arous-
ing any ill feeling in the breasts of the Northern men
against the Southern brethren. . . .

He first declared that the Southern slaveholders were
neither better nor worse than we of the North, and that
we of the North were no better than they. If we were
situated as they are, we should act no better than they.
If we were situated as they are, we should act and feel as
they do; and if they were situated as we are, they should

[1] Bloomington *Weekly Pantagraph*, Sept. 20, 1854. A longer and
different selection than is quoted here may be found in Lincoln,
Abraham, *New Letters and Papers of Lincoln*, comp. by P. M.
Angle (Boston 1930) p. 133-37.

act and feel as we do; and we never ought to lose sight
of this fact in discussing the subject. . . .

We have not space to give the Speaker's lucid argu-
ments against the Bill. They were irresistible. If the
"Little Giant" had been there, he would have felt all the
truth of that first half of the appellation, and realized
that he was the contrast of the latter half.

Another eye-witness account has been preserved to us by the description of Hon. James S.
Ewing, a lifetime resident of Bloomington and
U. S. Ambassador to Belgium during the years
1893-97: [2]

I heard Mr. Lincoln make a number of political
speeches. I heard his speech in the old court house in
1854, on the Kansas and Nebraska bill, in answer to the
speech of Mr. Douglas on the same subject, made a few
days before [in Chicago on Sept. 1st]. In this speech,
what impressed me most was that same wonderful power
of statement to which I have before referred. I can never
forget the manner in which he stated the causes and
events which led up to the enactment of the Missouri
Compromise; just what that compromise was, and how
it affected the question of slavery; the history of the
events and causes which led to the passage of the compromise of 1850; its constitutional elements; just what
the South got and just what the North got by it, and
how it was affected by the repeal of the other compromise bill. It seems to me I could almost repeat those
statements to-day, after a half century, so vivid was the
impression.

These descriptions of Lincoln's Bloomington
speech indicate that an address of unusual power

[2] Ewing, J. S. in Phillips, I. N., ed., *Op. cit.*, p. 50-51.

had been delivered. But its full importance is not realized until the descriptions are compared with Lincoln's extant speeches for possible identification. Then, and I have not seen this suggested elsewhere, then it is realized that this address is none other than the famous "Peoria Speech" which Lincoln delivered at Peoria on October 16, 1854, more than a month later. It is known that Lincoln gave substantially the same speech in Springfield on October 4th, which heretofore has been accepted as the time of its first delivery, but to Bloomington now must be given the honor of having heard it first. This was Lincoln's first great speech, in which he did, "for the first time in his life, publicly and in forthright words denounce slavery, and assert that it was incompatible with American institutions." [1] Contrary to popular impression Lincoln's hatred of slavery did not date from his early youth but was a plant of slow growth and the product of many vicissitudes. It was not until he had passed his 45th birthday that he came to this conclusion, and first publicly expressed it in this historic speech at Bloomington. (See Appendix I).

[1] Beveridge, A. J., *Op cit.,* vol. ii, p. 249.

XXI

ABOUT August 25, 1854, Stephen A. Douglas returned to Illinois from Washington, and in a speech at Chicago on September 1st he tried to justify himself for his efforts in behalf of the Nebraska Bill. When he arrived in Bloomington on September 26th, Jesse W. Fell laid before him and Lincoln his plan for joint debates between the two leaders. As Mr. Fell has left us a detailed written account of the circumstances attending this important proposal, I can do no better than quote it in full: [1]

Notwithstanding the high party-excitement referred to, his [Lincoln's] love of fair play shone out most conspicuously. Judge Douglas, fully apprised of the state of public feeling, had given out that on his return from Washington he would address the people on the exciting topic of the times, and in pursuance thereof a Democratic meeting was called at Bloomington on the 19th day of September, 1854.[2]   After conferring with our

[1] Fell, J. W. in Oldroyd, O. H., ed., *The Lincoln Memorial: Album-Immortelles* (New York 1883) p. 470-72.

[2] Mr. Fell seems to be mistaken in the date, as other evidence indicates September 26th to be the day for this event. See Angle, P. M., *Lincoln, 1854-1861* (Springfield, Ill. 1933) p. 39. In a letter to the author dated January 12, 1935, Mr. Angle says: "I am unable to cite specific authority which will rule out September 19th, 1854, as the date for the event which I have dated September 26th. However, the Illinois State Register, the Springfield Democratic organ, contained numerous references to speaking engagements of Douglas during September, while I have found none covering the 19th. It is apparent from others that about this time he was speaking in the counties adjacent to Cook County, and, therefore, outside the Bloomington area. Moreover, at the time when

Anti-Nebraska friends—as we were then commonly
called—I opened a correspondence with Mr. Lincoln,
resulting in his coming to Bloomington on that day, in
order to take notes and reply to Mr. Douglas, if the way
opened, on the same day, and if not, in the evening. This
fact became pretty widely known, and a very large meeting, composed of quite as many Anti-Nebraska men as
Democrats, met in the grove near town—no hall we
then had being sufficient to hold the crowd. In order that
the country people should have the benefit of the discussion, there was a universal desire, on the part of our
friends, that Lincoln as well as Douglas should be heard
in the day-time, and I had been requested to see Lincoln
on his arrival and get his approval that we propose to,
and *urge* upon the Judge to divide time, so as to have a
joint discussion.

With what little ability I could command, I did so,
emphasizing the fact that a large majority of those we
most desired to reach could not be heard unless this arrangement was made; and that in the absence of such an
agreement it would be quite difficult to restrain within
bounds the clamor of the people to hear him. I shall never
forget his very prompt and decisive reply, which was
substantially this: "Fell, this is not our meeting; it is

he was under the necessity of appearing as frequently as possible
in different parts of the state he would not have had two engagements in Bloomington a week apart. The fact that both Lincoln
and Douglas were in Bloomington on the 26th definitely rules out
the possibility of both of them having been there the 19th." On the
other hand, the McLean County Court at Bloomington ended its
fall sessions on Saturday, September 23rd, and Lincoln was
scheduled to attend the Court meetings at Metamora, Seat of Woodford County, starting on Monday, September 25th (Thomas, B. P.,
"Lincoln and the Courts, 1854-1861" in Abraham Lincoln Association, *Papers 1933,* p. 50, 64). Lincoln was in Bloomington attending Court on the 19th, but he could easily have left Metamora for
the day on the 26th. Judge Weldon says Lincoln was attending
Court in Bloomington on this occasion, but Mr. Fell says he arranged with Lincoln in advance to be present for this event.

Judge Douglas's meeting; he called it, and he and his friends have a right to control it. Notwithstanding all you say about our country people, and the great desire I have to talk to them, we must do nothing to defeat his object in calling it. He has heard of the great racket the passage of his Bill has kicked up, and he wants to set himself right with his people, a job not very easily done, you and I being the judges. Partly on this ground and partly to keep me from speaking, he will no doubt consume so much of the time that I'll have no chance till in the evening. I fully appreciate all you say about our country friends, and would like mighty well to talk to them on this subject. If Judge Douglas will give me a chance I will follow him out in the grove, but as he won't do this, I guess you may give it out, after he is done, that I will reply to him after candle lighting in the court-house."

This speech settled the matter. I will only add, in conclusion, our Anti-Nebraska friends were greatly disappointed at not getting his approval of some pretty active (perhaps I should say aggressive) demonstrations, to secure a division of time in the discussion; that, as we anticipated, the afternoon was consumed by the Judge; that so intense was the desire to hear Lincoln in the day-time, it was found quite difficult to repress a perfect avalanche of popular calls for our hero to be heard; and that, in the evening, he held forth at the old court-house to all that could get in it, or within hearing distance, in a most logical, eloquent and inspiring speech on the disturbed and perturbed condition of the country, and the consequent duties we owed to that country, and to a common humanity, in resisting, to the bitter end, this last aggression on Northern rights. In power and pathos, mingled with the playful and humorous, he seldom, if ever, acquitted himself more grandly.

It may not be amiss to say that before speaking com-

menced I called on Judge Douglas, who, as we had anticipated, politely declined the proffered debate; in doing
which he made some amusing, though good-natured, remarks about the uncertain character of our party, which
in truth was, at that time, far from being of a very compact or coherent order, either in name or creed.

Mr. Fell's last paragraph is highly abridged, and
thus leaves out the interesting and important details of his conversation with Judge Douglas.
Fortunately, this omission is supplied by more
than one eye-witness to the proceedings, from one
of whom I quote the following account: [1]

The first time I met him [Lincoln] was in September,
1854, at Bloomington; and I was introduced to him by
Judge Douglas, who was then making a campaign in
defense of the Kansas-Nebraska bill. Mr. Lincoln was
attending court, and called to see the Judge. They
talked very pleasantly about old times and things, and
during the conversation the Judge broadened the hospi-
talities of the occasion by asking him to drink something.
Mr. Lincoln declined very politely, when the Judge said:
"Why, do you belong to the temperance society?" He
said:

"I do *not* in theory, but I do in fact, belong to the temperance society, in this, to wit, that I do not drink anything, and have not done so for a very many years."

Shortly after he retired, Mr. J. W. Fell, then and now
a leading citizen of Illinois, came into the room, with a
proposition that Mr. Lincoln and Mr. Douglas have a
discussion, remarking that there were a great many

[1] Weldon, Lawrence, in Rice, A. T., ed., *Op. cit.,* p. 198-99. *Cf.*
Weldon, Lawrence, in Chicago *Tribune,* Feb. 9, 1902 and Bloom-
ington *Pantagraph,* Feb. 10, 1902; Stevenson, A. E., *Op. cit.,* p. 8-9;
Ewing, J. S. in Phillips, I. N., ed., *Op cit.,* p. 52-53, 55-57.

people in the city, that the question was of great public importance, and that it would afford the crowd the luxury of listening to the acknowledged champions of both sides. As soon as the proposition was made it could be seen that the Judge was irritated. He inquired of Mr. Fell, with some majesty of manner: "Whom does Mr. Lincoln represent in this campaign—is he an Abolitionist or an Old Line Whig?"

Mr. Fell replied that he was an Old Line Whig.

"Yes," said Douglas, "I am now in the region of the Old Line Whig. When I am in Northern Illinois I am assailed by an Abolitionist, when I get to the center I am attacked by an Old Line Whig, and when I go to Southern Illinois I am beset by an Anti-Nebraska Democrat. I can't hold the Whig responsible for anything the Abolitionist says, and can't hold the Anti-Nebraska Democrat responsible for the positions of either. It looks to me like dogging a man all over the State. If Mr. Lincoln wants to make a speech he had better get a crowd of his own; for I most respectfully decline to hold a discussion with him."

Mr. Lincoln had nothing to do with the challenge except perhaps to say he would discuss the question with Judge Douglas. He was not aggressive in the defense of his doctrines or enunciation of his opinions, but he was brave and fearless in the protection of what he believed to be the right.

Mr. Fell's plan for joint discussions between Lincoln and Douglas failed, but he did not give up the idea. However, "he was the first man to suggest it. From 1854 to 1858 he continued to urge it, and to Mr. Jesse W. Fell, more than to any other man, is due the credit of bringing about those great debates, the full influence of which, upon

Mr. Lincoln's fortunes, the events of history and the fate of the nation, no man is wise enough to know." [1]

Until the year 1935 no printed account of Lincoln's speech on this occasion in Bloomington was ever found, but early in that year a three-column account was found in the Peoria *Weekly Republican* for October 6, 1854, and reprinted for Lincoln students.[2] This speech contains passages which cover the same ground which we have learned were in his Bloomington speech of two weeks earlier and paralleled in his "Peoria Speech" of three weeks later. On the other hand, there are passages which are not to be found in the other two addresses, and on the whole this speech is much less like the "Peoria Speech" than the Bloomington speech of September 12th. This, then, was Lincoln's second reply to Douglas before his answer in Springfield on October 4th, and both of them were delivered in Bloomington.

XXII

THE Convention in Springfield on October 4th and 5th was the earliest attempt in Illinois to organize a State Republican Party on the basis of

[1] Ewing, J. S. in Phillips, I. N., *Op cit.*, p. 57.
[2] East, E. E., ed., "A Newly Discovered Speech of Lincoln" in Illinois State Historical Society, *Journal,* vol. xxviii (Springfield, Ill. 1935-36) p. 65-77.

opposition to the Nebraska law.[1] Although only twenty-six delegates attended, a platform was adopted and a Bloomington man was nominated for the office of State Treasurer. A Republican State Central Committee was appointed, which included Abraham Lincoln, but he took no part in the Convention and refused to serve on the Committee. He was a Whig by party affiliation, and he expected his party to take a stand against the Nebraska bill. The Convention failed in its object, however, and the Republican Party did not materialize—the time was not yet ripe. Over a month later Lincoln received a letter from Ichabod Codding, abolitionist and Chairman of the State Central Committee, which drew from him the following reply: [2]

Springfield, *November 27, 1854.*

I. Codding, Esq.
Dear Sir:

Your note of the 13th requesting my attendance on the Republican State Central Committee, on the 17th instant at Chicago, was, owing to my absence from home, received on the evening of that day (17th) only. While I have pen in hand allow me to say I have been perplexed some to understand why my name was placed on that committee. I was not consulted on the subject, nor was I apprised of the appointment until I discovered it by accident two or three weeks afterward. I suppose my opposition to the principle of slavery is as strong as

[1] Selby, Paul, "Republican State Convention, Springfield, Ill., October 4-5, 1854" in McLean Co. Historical Soc., *Op. cit.,* vol. iii, p. 43-47.

[2] Lincoln, Abraham, *Complete Works,* vol. ii, p. 264.

that of any member of the Republican party, but I have
also supposed that the extent to which I feel authorized
to carry that opposition, practically, was not at all satisfactory to that party. The leading men who organized
that party were present on the 4th of October at the
discussion between Douglas and myself at Springfield,
and had full opportunity to not misunderstand my position. Do I misunderstand them? Please write and inform me.

Yours truly,

A. LINCOLN.

As there have been rival claims for the honor of
being the birthplace of the Republican Party, a
few words on the subject might not be out of order. Ripon, Wisconsin, claims that a meeting was
held there as early as February 28, 1854, which
adopted a resolution to form a "Republican" Party if the Senate should pass the Nebraska Bill.
The Senate did pass the measure and another
meeting was called on March 3rd, but no permanent results came from it. Jackson, Michigan, held
the first "Republican" State Convention, on July
6, 1854, but its influence died in 1860. So while
Wisconsin and Michigan can both claim earlier
"Republican" meetings than Illinois, they had no
more permanent result than did the State Convention at Springfield, Illinois. In fact, the Republican Party of today, with unbroken history, was
not founded in 1854! When and where the Party
was born remains to be told further on.

XXIII

ON November 7, 1854, Abraham Lincoln was
elected to the Legislature on the Whig ticket
against his will. But three months later an election for United States Senator was to be held,
and since the law did not allow a member of the
Legislature to become a Senator Mr. Lincoln resigned from that body hoping for the later election. However, on February 8, 1855, when the
election was held, Lincoln was defeated and he
turned over to Lyman Trumbull the votes he had
received, which helped to elect the latter candidate. In her account of this campaign, [1] Miss Ida
M. Tarbell makes another error when she places
the Senatorial election in November, 1854, and
fails entirely to mention Lincoln's election to the
Legislature at that time.

XXIV

JUDGE David Davis of Bloomington was reelected to his leadership of the Eighth Judicial
Circuit in June, 1855, for a period of six years.
During all that time since his first election, Lincoln followed him from county to county as leading lawyer of the circuit. Mr. John H. Wickizer,

[1] Tarbell, I. M., *In the Footsteps of the Lincolns* (New York
1924) p. 325.

Left—Marker of Eighth Judicial Circuit, Courthouse Square, Bloomington, Illinois.

Below—This tablet is placed on Major's Hall, Bloomington, Illinois.

resident of Bloomington and its third Mayor, tells a story that occurred about this time: "In 1855 Mr. Lincoln and myself were travelling by buggy from Woodford County Court to Bloomington, Ill.; and, in passing through a little grove we suddenly heard the terrific squealing of a little pig near by us. Quick as thought Mr. Lincoln leaped out of the buggy, seized a club, pounced upon the old sow, and beat her lustily: she was in the act of eating one of her young ones. Thus he saved the pig, and then remarked, 'By Jing! the unnatural old brute shall not devour her own progeny!' This, I think, was his first proclamation of freedom." [1]

XXV

ON the night of October 16, 1855, a fire destroyed the entire block facing the south side of the Court House Square in Bloomington, which burned the buildings of Kersey H. Fell and Dr. C. Wakefield. Hardly before the bricks were cold, however, new buildings were in course of construction, and a year later the first four-story buildings in the town were completed. The new frontage, to commemorate the resurrection from the ashes of the burned buildings, was appropriately named "Phoenix Block." In it were the drug store of R. Thompson & Co., Dr. Wakefield's former store sold to his brother-in-law, and

[1] Lamon, W. H., *Op. cit.*, p. 325.

the law office of Kersey H. Fell, the latter over
the Home Bank. The fire had destroyed the print-
ing plant of Dr. C. Wakefield's Democratic newspaper, the *Illinois State Bulletin,* as well as that
of the Anti-Nebraskan paper, the *Pantagraph,*
but the latter was the only one that survived.
Though prominent Democrats offered to help his
paper financially, and even to buy it outright, Dr.
Wakefield refused to rehabilitate it. Dr. Wakefield was the largest single loser by the fire and the
paper was one of his greatest assets, but since its
establishment in 1851 he had become a close friend
and admirer of Abraham Lincoln and had been
won over by him to Anti-Nebraska views. Thus
he allowed his paper to die. Accordingly what
might have been a powerful political enemy of
Lincoln was removed, and in its place he gained
an ardent and influential friend.

XXVI

DURING the course of the great fire of October 16, 1855, a man by the name of Samuel
G. Fleming was badly injured by the falling of a
wall and one of his legs was fractured. He was
treated for his injuries by two leading physicians,
Doctors Eli K. Crothers and Thomas P. Rogers.
By the time his fractured leg had healed he found
that the injured member was shorter than his good
leg, and he filed suit in the McLean County Cir-

cuit Court against the doctors for malpractice on March 28, 1856. The attorneys for the plaintiff were the firms of Swett & Orme and Gridley & Wickizer, and those for the defendants were Brier & Birch with the assistance of Abraham Lincoln. Mr. Lincoln was an old friend of the Crothers family, and a nurse who had formerly brought up the Lincoln boys in Springfield was then in charge of the Crothers household. It was natural, then, that Lincoln should take part in the defense of Doctors Crothers and Rogers.

The case was heard many times in the McLean County Circuit Court under Judge David Davis, with no satisfactory decision. On April 10, 1857, the jury was discharged when it failed to agree after having been out eighteen hours.[1] On September 8, 1857, Dr. Crothers filed an affidavit for continuance of the case, in which he said that "one of his counsel, Mr. Lincoln, is not and cannot be in attendance at this court because of his necessary attendance on the Circuit Court of the United States now in session at Chicago." The case continued in Bloomington until December 21, 1857, when Judge David Davis, on the motion of the defendants, entered an order for changing the venue from McLean County to the Circuit Court of Logan County at the town of Lincoln.

For the defense of the case, Dr. Crothers coached Lincoln in the physiology of bone repair, in the young when there is a plentiful natural sup-

[1] *Bloomington Daily Pantagraph,* April 11, 1857.

ply of organic material in the bones and in the old
when the organic material has been absorbed and
the bones are brittle. These examples were illustrated in court by the use of chicken bones which
had been prepared by Dr. Crothers. But Lincoln
could not remember the technical descriptions,
and in referring to the bone of a young chicken
he said "this bone has the starch all taken out of it
—as it is in childhood." [1] He asked Mr. Fleming,
"Can you walk at all?" To which Fleming replied, "Yes, but my leg is short so I have to limp."
Lincoln impressed the jury by retorting, "Well!
What I would advise *you* to do is to get down on
your knees and thank your Heavenly Father and
also these two Doctors that you have any legs to
stand on at all." In other words, most doctors
would have amputated so badly injured a leg.

On March 15, 1858, Judge David Davis presiding over the Logan County Court, ordered
that the case be dismissed "as per agreement on
file." Unfortunately, the agreement referred to
is missing from the papers and files of the Logan
County Courthouse. It is possible that Lincoln
wrote it and that it is now in some private col-
lection. This order ended the case.[2]

[1] This and the following conversation are included in a letter to
the author from Miss Lulu M. Crothers, daughter of Dr. Crothers
and sister of Miss Rachel Crothers, the well-known dramatist,
dated October 30, 1935.

[2] I am indebted to Judge Lawrence B. Stringer, of the Logan
County Court at Lincoln, Ill., for valuable transcripts from the
records of this case in the Logan County Courthouse. Aside from
an incomplete and partly erroneous account of this case in Shutes,
M. H., *Lincoln and the Doctors* (New York 1933), this is the first
publication it has had.

XXVII

HAVING held his two Bloomington lots since he purchased them in October, 1851, Lincoln sold them on April 12, 1856 to a man named Francis Thomas for the sum of $400, thus making $75 on his investment.[1] If Lincoln originally intended to live in Bloomington, Mrs. Lincoln probably decided to remain in Springfield for its greater social and political opportunities. The lots were purchased in 1887 by Dr. Marie Louise Crothers, mother of Miss Rachel Crothers, the well-known playwright, whose sister now lives in the Crothers homestead on the site.

XXVIII

LATE in December, 1855, Paul Selby, Editor of the Morgan (now Jacksonville) *Journal* published an editorial suggesting a meeting of the Anti-Nebraska Editors of the State for the purpose of deciding upon a policy for the year 1856. Twenty-five papers responded, including the Bloomington *Pantagraph,* and an "Editorial Convention" was held in Decatur on February 22nd.[2] Abraham Lincoln came up from Springfield and assisted the Committee on Resolutions

[1] McLean Co. Court *Deeds,* Book xxvii, p. 686. Filed May 13, 1856. Recorded May 20, 1856.

[2] Selby, Paul, "The Editorial Convention of 1856" in Illinois State Historical Soc., *Journal,* vol. v (1912-13) 343-49.

to draw up a platform, which chiefly protested against the introduction of slavery into free territory and demanded the restoration of the Missouri Compromise. "The platform as a whole," said Paul Selby in 1900, "amounted to a declaration of the most conservative Republicanism, and the foresight of its authors was indicated by the reiteration of every feature of it, in subsequent years, in the utterances of state and national conventions of the party."[1] But more important even was the following resolution, which was adopted:[2]

Resolved, That this convention recommend a state delegate convention to be held on Thursday, the 29th day of May next, in the city of Bloomington, and that the state central committee be requested to fix the ratio of representation for that convention, and take such steps as may seem desirable to bring about a full representation from the whole state.

Thus was started the machinery which resulted in the organization of the Republican Party in the State of Illinois and in the nation at large.

The State Central Committee of Illinois issued the following call, which was published at Bloomington in the *Weekly Pantagraph* of May 14, 1856:

ANTI-NEBRASKA STATE CONVENTION.

A State Convention of the Anti-Nebraska party of Illinois will be held in the City of Bloomington, on

[1] McLean Co. Historical Society, *Op. cit.*, vol. iii, p. 38.
[2] *Ibid*, vol. iii, p. 38.

Thursday, the 29th day of May, 1856, for the purpose of choosing candidates for State officers, appointing delegates to the National Convention, and transacting such other business as may properly come before the body.

The committee have adopted as the basis of representation the ratio of one delegate to every 6,000 inhabitants, and an additional delegate for every fractional number of 2,000 and over; but counties that contain less than 6,000 inhabitants are entitled to one delegate.

WM. B. OGDEN	THOS. J. PICKETT
S. M. CHURCH	G. D. A. PARKS
E. A. DUDLEY	W. H. HERNDON
R. J. OGLESBY	JOE GILLESPIE
IRA O. WILKINSON	D. L. PHILLIPS

STATE CENTRAL COMMITTEE.

Beneath this call was printed another call for the voters of McLean County, who were favorable to the Anti-Nebraska movement, to meet at the Court House in Bloomington on May 17th to select three delegates to the State Convention. The mass meeting was held according to schedule, and James Gilmore, Dr. Harrison Noble, and William W. Orme were elected delegates, and Green B. Larrison, David Cheney, and A. T. Briscoe were chosen alternates. The State Convention was not called "Republican" for two reasons: first, because the Republican Party was not yet founded; and secondly, because Senator Douglas had tried to give the word "Republican" a bad name by prefixing the word "Black" whenever he referred to it. So the call was for an Anti-Nebraska Convention, which had a definite meaning and invited all shades of opposition to the Nebraska Bill of Senator Douglas.

XXIX

THE day of the Convention in Bloomington, May 29, 1856, was fair and warm.[1] From early morning the normally quiet city of 6,000 inhabitants was crowded and excited. Every train that came, no matter from what part of the State, brought increasing numbers of people. The Pike House, on the corner of Center and North (now Monroe) streets, was crowded with delegates, and was the scene of many speeches from its balconies. Lincoln was one of the speakers, and in his address he used his now famous saying, perhaps for the first time: "You can fool some of the people all of the time, and all of the people some of the time, but you can't fool all of the people all of the time." [2] Lincoln had arrived the day before, as a delegate from Sangamon County, because his partner Herndon had signed his name to the call for delegates without consulting him—but he later gave his consent to attend. The previous afternoon Lincoln and Henry C. Whitney had walked to the "Alton" station to meet the delegates from Chicago, and on the way Lincoln had

[1] Cunningham, J. O., "The Bloomington Convention of 1856 and Those Who Participated in It" in Illinois State Historical Soc., *Transactions,* vol. x (1906) p. 101-10.

[2] Morgan, R. P. in Phillips, I. N., ed., *Op. cit.,* p. 102-03.

stopped in "a very diminutive jewelry shop" and bought his first pair of spectacles, for which he paid 37½ cents. He told Whitney "he had got to be forty-seven years old, and 'kinder' needed them." [1] The Convention was held in Major's Hall, over the grocery store of Humphrey & Wakefield (Elisha Wakefield, brother of Dr. C. Wakefield), on the corner of East and Front streets. The meeting was called to order at 10 A. M., and after a committee was appointed to nominate permanent officers of the Convention and Mr. James S. Emory of Kansas delivered an address, Colonel William H. Bissell was nominated for Governor and Francis A. Hoffman for Lieutenant-Governor amid great enthusiasm. However, Mr. Hoffman was found to be ineligible, and John Wood was nominated instead. Following a speech by the Hon. Richard Yates the Convention adjourned at noon for luncheon. The afternoon session convened at two P. M., and committees which had been appointed in the morning session reported. Abraham Lincoln had been appointed a member of the committee to report to the convention suitable candidates for the other state offices. He was also nominated one of the presidential electors to the national convention, for the state at large, by the committee appointed for that purpose. Lincoln's committee, to recommend persons for candidates for vacant

[1] Whitney, H. C., *Life on the Circuit with Lincoln* (Boston 1892) p. 75.

state offices, reported the following: For Secretary of State, Ozias M. Hatch, of Pike County; for State Treasurer, James Miller, of Bloomington; for State Auditor, Jesse K. Dubois, of Lawrence; and for Superintendent of Common Schools, William H. Powell, of Peoria. Lincoln himself was among the delegates from the Sixth District who were elected to attend the national Anti-Nebraska Convention, which was to meet June 17th at Philadelphia, but he did not go when the time came.

At about four o'clock the committee to prepare resolutions expressive of the intent of the convention, reported, and the result was unanimously adopted. The first six resolutions were as follows: [1]

Resolved, That foregoing all former differences of opinion upon other questions, we pledge ourselves to unite in opposition to the present administration, and to the party which upholds and supports it, and to use all honorable and constitutional means to wrest the government from the unworthy hands which now control it, and bring it back in its administration to the principles and practices of Washington, Jefferson and their great and good compatriots of the revolution.

Resolved, That we hold, in accordance with the opinions and practices of all the great statesmen of all parties, for the first sixty years of the administration of the government, that, under the constitution, congress possesses full power to prohibit slavery in the territories; and that whilst we will maintain all constitutional rights

[1] McLean Co. Historical Society, *Op. cit.,* vol. iii, p. 160-61.

of the south, we also hold that justice, humanity, the principles of freedom as expressed in our Declaration of Independence, and our national constitution and the purity and perpetuity of our government, require that power should be exerted to prevent the extension of slavery into territories heretofore free.

Resolved, That the repeal of the Missouri Compromise was unwise, unjust and injurious; an open and aggravated violation of the plighted faith of the states, and that the attempt of the present administration to force slavery into Kansas against the known wishes of the legal voters of that territory, is an arbitrary and tyrannous violation of the rights of the people to govern themselves, and that we will strive by all constitutional means to secure to Kansas and Nebraska the legal guarantee against slavery of which they were deprived at the cost of the violation of the plighted faith of the nation.

Resolved, That we are devoted to the Union, and will to the last extremity, defend it against the efforts now being made by the disunionists of the administration to compass its dissolution, and that we will support the constitution of the United States in all its provisions; regarding it as the sacred bond of our Union, and the only safeguard for the preservation of the rights of ourselves and our posterity.

Resolved, That we are in favor of the immediate admission of Kansas as a member of this confederacy, under the constitution adopted by the people of said territory.

Resolved, That the spirit of our institutions, as well as the constitution of our country guarantee the liberty of conscience as well as political freedom, and that we will proscribe no one, by legislation or otherwise, on account of religious opinions, or in consequence of place of birth.

The essence of this "platform" was the unification of the people, regardless of previous party affiliations, prevention of the extension of slavery, the preservation of the Union, and the observance of religious and racial liberty. After a State Central Committee had been appointed, which included Asahel Gridley of Bloomington, the following resolution was adopted:

Resolved, That this convention recommend every town in every county in the state to form Anti-Nebraska clubs, for the purpose of effecting a thorough organization of the party prior to the ensuing election.

Thus no stone was left unturned to make effective the policies of the convention.

After the committees had all reported, the speaking commenced. First, Mr. Orville H. Browning, of Quincy, spoke, and he was followed by Owen Lovejoy, of Princeton. Then came Abraham Lincoln, who made *the* speech of the occasion. He spoke for an hour and a half amid the greatest excitement and enthusiasm. He urged unity, and the convention, composed of Abolitionists, Free Soil Whigs and "Anti-Nebraska" Democrats, became as one man—Republican. He made the first public utterance of the possibility of war, but urged that the use of ballots at the November election might prevent the later use of bullets. He gave public expression for the first time to the principle that the nation cannot exist half-slave and half-free—the principle which he

had formulated in Bloomington two years previously—thus anticipating his famous "House
Divided" speech at Springfield two years later.[1]
The climax of the speech was reached when Lincoln, towering above the audience, cried: "We will
say to the Southern disunionists, We won't go
out of the Union, and you SHAN'T!!" The effect was electric. Although the hall was dotted
with reporters from newspapers all over the country, each one after the speech was chagrined to
find that he had been so enthralled by the address
that he had failed to report it. Thus it is known
as the "Lost Speech," and though forty years
later Mr. H. C. Whitney wrote out what he
thought Lincoln had said, most of Lincoln's Illinois friends still consider the speech lost.[2] Lincoln was afterwards urged to write out the speech,
but he always refused, saying it was impossible
for him to remember what he had said and how he
had said it. As a matter of fact, it was generally
thought that Lincoln was glad that the speech
was lost, as it was too radical for the country as a
whole at that time. However, many years later

[1] Herndon, W. H., *Op. cit.,* p. 325-26. Mr. Dickey is mistaken
about the Pike House, as Lincoln and he stayed at the home of
Judge Davis on this occasion (Whitney, H. C., *Op. cit.,* p.73).

[2] Whitney, H. C. and Medill, Joseph, "Lincoln's Lost Speech" in
McClure's Magazine, vol. vii (1896) 319-31; also in Tarbell, I. M.,
The Life of Abraham Lincoln. 2 vols. (New York 1900) vol. ii,
p. 306-21. In addition see McLean Co. Historical Society, *Op. cit.,*
vol. iii, p. 180; Phillips, I. N., *Abraham Lincoln: a Short Study of
a Great Man and his Work* (Bloomington, Ill. 1901) p. 57-60; and
Abraham Lincoln Association, *Bulletin,* no. xxi (Springfield, Ill.
1930) 3-5.

several of the men who were present said they considered this speech the greatest of his life. As a typical expression, ten years later Herndon stated the following in a lecture:[1]

I have heard or read all of Mr. Lincoln's great speeches, and I give it as my opinion that the Bloomington speech was the grand effort of his life. Heretofore he had simply argued the slavery question on grounds of policy,—the statesman's grounds,—never reaching the question of the radical and the eternal right. Now he was newly baptized and freshly born; he had the fervor of a new convert; the smothered flame broke out; enthusiasm unusual to him blazed up; his eyes were aglow with an inspiration; he felt justice; his heart was alive to the right; his sympathies, remarkably deep for him, burst forth, and he stood before the throne of the eternal Right. His speech was full of fire and energy and force; it was logic; it was pathos; it was enthusiasm; it was justice, equity, truth, and right set ablaze by the divine fires of a soul maddened by the wrong; it was hard, heavy, knotty, gnarly, backed with wrath. I attempted for about fifteen minutes as was usual with me then to take notes, but at the end of that time I threw pen and paper away and lived only in the inspiration of the hour. If Mr. Lincoln was six feet four inches high usually, at Bloomington that day he was seven feet, and inspired at that. From that day to the day of his death he stood firm in the right. He felt his great cross, had his great idea, nursed it, kept it, taught it to others, in his fidelity bore witness of it to his death, and finally sealed it with his precious blood.

As evidence of the powerful impression made by

[1] Herndon, W. H., *Op. cit.,* p. 312-13.

Lincoln that day in Bloomington, thirty-two years after the event Herndon wrote: [1]

The foregoing paragraph, used by me in a lecture in 1866, may to the average reader seem somewhat vivid in description, besides inclining to extravagance in imagery, yet although more than twenty years have passed since it was written I have never seen the need of altering a single sentence. I still adhere to the substantial truthfulness of the scene as described.

Although it was about 7 o'clock when Lincoln finished his speech, the audience of 1,000 people refused to leave and called for an address by Burton C. Cook, of Ottawa, who complied and ended the convention. Among the men who were present at the Convention were Abraham Lincoln, future President of the United States; John M. Palmer, later Governor of Illinois and U. S. Senator; O. H. Browning, later U. S. Senator, Secretary of the Interior, and Acting Attorney-General of the United States; Richard Yates, later Governor of Illinois and U. S. Senator; Richard J. Oglesby, later three times Governor of Illinois and U. S. Senator; David Davis, later Justice of the U. S. Supreme Court, U. S. Senator, and Acting Vice-President of the United States; John L. Routt, later Governor of Colorado; Norman B. Judd, who later nominated Lincoln for the Presidency and became a U. S. foreign minister; John G. Nicolay, Lincoln's future Private Secretary and Biographer; and several

[1] Herndon, W. H., *Op. cit.*, p. 313.

future Congressmen and members of the Illinois Legislature. Needless to say Jesse W. Fell and Leonard Swett were also there. Truly an impressive gathering!

The Bloomington Convention was called as an Anti-Nebraska meeting and ended by founding and organizing the Republican Party in Illinois and the United States. The name "Republican" was not assumed by it at the time, but was soon after adopted, and there is no question about the Republican nature of the Convention. The numerous county and Congressional District conventions which met in 1854 and generally adopted the name of "Republican," had sent delegates to the Bloomington Convention. The State ticket nominated by the Convention for the November election was known as "Republican" during the campaign. Lincoln's "Lost Speech" marked the real birth of the Republican Party, and it was the most momentous event in Lincoln's life—when he threw off the old order of things and became a Republican himself. Up to that meeting he had been a Whig, but now he knew that the Whig Party had served its usefulness and was doomed. Lincoln's speech at once made him the acknowledged leader of the new party in Illinois, and later throughout the nation, for he was now on the track which lead to the Presidency of the United States. That Lincoln himself considered the Bloomington Convention the organizer of the Republican Party is evidenced by the opening of his debate with Douglas at Freeport, August 27, 1858: "I have supposed myself, since the organization of the Republican party at Bloomington, in May, 1856, bound as a party man by the platforms of the party then and since." [1] He thus eliminated all previous attempts to organize a Republican Party, including the 1854 meetings in Illinois. In fact, since the Bloomington Convention is the only one which furnishes an unbroken continuity, through the State election of 1856 and the National election of 1860, to the present day, we may say what later became the National Republican Party was born in Bloomington, Illinois, on May 29, 1856.

The great difference existing between Bloomington and Springfield, Lincoln's home city, in loyalty to Republicanism and to Lincoln himself, is admirably illustrated by what followed the rousing Bloomington Convention. A few days later Lincoln and his law-partner, Herndon, called a meeting in the Court House at Springfield to ratify the action taken by the Convention at Bloomington. "After the usual efforts to draw a crowd, however, only three persons had temerity enough to attend," says Herndon. "They were Lincoln, the writer, and a courageous man named John Pain. Lincoln, in answer to the 'deafening calls' for a speech, responded that the meeting was larger than he *knew* it would be, and that while he knew that he himself and his partner would attend

[1] Lincoln, Abraham, *Complete Works,* vol. iii, p. 272.

he was not sure any one else would, and yet another man had been found brave enough to come out." [1]

About two weeks later, however, on June 10th, another ratification meeting was called at the Court House in Springfield, which was attended by two hundred people. Abraham Lincoln, John M. Palmer, and others addressed the meeting, but they were received with coldness if not hostility. Giving up Springfield as a failure, Lincoln then canvassed the State, and made about fifty speeches for the Republican cause. [2]

The first National Anti-Nebraska Convention was held in Philadelphia on June 17, 1856, and delegates were sent from all over the country. Delegates to represent Illinois had been chosen at the Bloomington Convention in May. Lincoln received 110 votes for the nomination of Vice-President of the United States, obtaining the total votes of the Illinois delegation. The successful nominees were John C. Frémont for President and William L. Dayton for Vice-President, who composed the first National Republican ticket. For the National Convention, like the Illinois Convention at Bloomington, began as Anti-Nebraskan and ended as Republican.

[1] Herndon, W. H., *Op. cit.,* p. 314-15. In spite of Mr. Angle's note to this statement, I see no reason to make it the sole exception to Herndon's veracity. I agree with Beveridge (*Op. cit.,* vol. ii, p. 382, 384) that there were two meetings.

[2] Wiley, E. W., "Lincoln in the campaign of 1856" in Illinois State Historical Soc., *Journal,* vol. xxii (1929-30) p. 582-92.

XXX

THE Republican campaign before the election in November, 1856, brought to Bloomington three rousing mass meetings, at two of which Abraham Lincoln spoke within a five-day interval. The first meeting, held on Friday, September 12th, was reported as follows: [1]

Friday night, a large Republican meeting was held in Major's Hall—a considerable number of ladies present among the rest. Hon. A. Lincoln addressed the audience in a speech of great eloquence and power. He showed up the position of the Fillmore party in fine style, both as to its prospects of success, and as to the propriety of supporting a candidate whose greatest recommendation, as urged by his supporters themselves, is that he is *neutral* upon the one only great political question of the times. He pointed out in regular succession, the several steps taken by the Administration in regard to slavery in the Territories, from the repeal of the Missouri Compromise down to the latest Border Ruffian invasion of Kansas, and the inevitable tendency of each and all of them to effect the spread of slavery over that country; showed the official endorsement of the Administration by the Democratic party in the Cincinnati Convention, and the openly avowed position of the Southern wing of the party on the subject of slavery-extension; contrasting all this with the assertion of our Northern Democratic speakers, that they are not in favor of the extension of slavery, with a clearness and force we have never heard excelled, and which must have made the *honest*

[1] Bloomington *Weekly Pantagraph,* Sept. 17, 1856.

Democrats, if any such there were present, feel as if they had received an eye-opener.

The next occasion was on the following Tuesday, September 16th. In the afternoon a Democratic meeting was held in front of the Pike House, which was attended by Lincoln and Swett. The meeting was interrupted, however, by the passing of a wagon decorated with a Frémont and Dayton banner. The Democratic organ in its account said: [1]

The rowdies that were posted on the outside of the crowd raised a shout for Frémont, and a rowdyish rabble started for the wagon. By the interference of some Democrats, together with Messrs. Lincoln and Swett, they were prevented from entering the ground. So they contented themselves with shouting and otherwise disturbing the meeting. To the honor and credit of our Republican friends in Bloomington, we will state that this disgraceful, ungentlemanly, and cowardly attempt to interrupt a public meeting originated in the low, groveling, and contemptible brain of a certain doctor of Cheney's Grove, followed by a gang of lesser lights, including a certain not very high-toned doctor of this city, with other rowdies picked up on their way whose names we might mention, and *may* take occasion to do so yet; but will forbear for the present.

On the evening of the same day, according to the Republican organ, "Mr. Lincoln had a crowded room-full at Major's Hall, who listened with intense interest to a most masterly speech, in which

[1] Bloomington *National Flag,* Sept. 19, 1856, quoted in Sandburg, Carl, *Op cit.,* vol. ii, p. 87.

he tore the day-time speeches of the Bucks at their great meeting into ribbons." [1]

The third important Republican meeting in Bloomington was held on October 9, 1856, with a big celebration. All that was lacking was the inspiring presence of Abraham Lincoln, who was speaking in Peoria. The enthusiastic account of the *Pantagraph* was as follows: [2]

GREAT REPUBLICAN MEETING AT BLOOMINGTON.

SPLENDID PROCESSION.   10,000 PEOPLE OUT.

Thursday last, 9th instant, was a glorious day for the Republican Cause in McLean County. The people were out in their strength, and their numbers and enthusiasm, the eloquent appeals of the orators on the ground, and the brilliant display of the long procession with its numerous flags and banners, cheered and inspired the hearts of the friends of freedom and gave earnest of the strength of the rightful cause in this section of the Prairie State. . . . The extreme pressure of demands upon speakers in every part of the state, and indeed of the Union, deprived us of the presence of many on whom we had counted. Messrs. Trumbull and Lincoln were engaged at the mass meeting in Peoria, and others were doing vigorous battle for the cause elsewhere.

The immediate success of the Republican Party founded in Bloomington is seen by the result of the State election held in November. The entire ticket nominated by the Bloomington Convention of May 29th was elected by large plur-

[1] Bloomington *Weekly Pantagraph*, Sept. 24, 1856.
[2] Bloomington *Weekly Pantagraph*, Oct. 15, 1856.

alities, the largest vote going to James Miller, the only Bloomington candidate. Thus the new party at once came into power in the State of Illinois, and started on the road which lead to national success in 1860.

XXXI

ON February 11, 1857, the Eighth Judicial Circuit of Illinois was reduced to the five counties of McLean, Logan, DeWitt, Champaign and Vermilion (20 *Session Laws,* p. 12). Although Lincoln's home county of Sangamon was thereby removed from the Eighth Circuit, and attached to the Eighteenth Circuit, Lincoln continued his law practice with Judge Davis. And contrary to the statements of most Lincoln biographers, his circuit riding did not end with 1857 but continued to within a few weeks of his nomination for the Presidency in 1860. Of all the counties which ever made up the Eighth Judicial Circuit, from its organization in 1839 to Lincoln's leaving it in 1860, only McLean (county seat, Bloomington) and Logan counties enjoyed Lincoln's presence the entire period.

XXXII

A LAW trial important both to Abraham Lincoln and Leonard Swett, one which has been neglected by Lincoln biographers, took place in Bloomington during the spring of 1857. It was known as the case of the People vs. Wyant, and was one of the first instances in the country where the plea of insanity extenuated the crime of murder. The circumstances were these: in June, 1855, Ason Rusk and Isaac Wyant quarrelled over a line boundary in DeWitt County, near Clinton, and Rusk shot Wyant in the arm. The result was that chloroform was administered to Wyant and his arm was amputated. After he had recovered from the operation, Wyant, seeing Rusk in the County Clerk's office in Clinton, on October 12, 1855, shot him four times to death in broad daylight and in the presence of several people. Rusk was about 23 years old, and Wyant was about 34. By a change of venue, the trial of Wyant for murder was ordered at Bloomington for September 10, 1856, but was postponed on account of the necessary absence of an important witness for the defendant. The trial formally opened at the Circuit Court in Bloomington, before Judge David Davis and a jury, on Tuesday, March 31, 1857. Abraham Lincoln, Ward H. Lamon, C. H. Moore and Harvey Hogg, of Bloomington, conducted the prosecution, and Leonard Swett and William W. Orme, law partners of Bloomington, led the defense. On the opening day Lincoln presented the evidence for the prosecution, and made out a clear *prima facie* case by the witnesses, the evidence for the State closing that evening. On Wednesday, April 1st, Mr. Swett opened the case for the defense with a long and powerful speech.

The fact of the killing was not denied, the defense resting its case on the ground of insanity. Several medical witnesses were examined on this point, including Dr. Andrew J. McFarland, of the State Insane Asylum, and Doctors Roe, Spencer and Parke of Bloomington. The defense brought out that two of Wyant's uncles were insane; that Wyant's insanity was caused by an overdose of chloroform administered to him when his arm was amputated; that before his operation he was a fine courageous man and that afterward his whole nature changed and he became a coward. On the following day the defense completed the presentation of its evidence. On Friday, April 3rd, the evidence was summed up by Mr. Hogg, for the prosecution, and Mr. Orme, for the defense. The next day Abraham Lincoln made the closing argument for the prosecution in a powerful speech lasting from one o'clock until nearly six in the evening. The case then went to the jury, and sometime after midnight when the jury agreed the Court was called together and a verdict of acquittal was given with the recommendation that the prisoner be confined in an insane asylum. The Court accepted the verdict, and Wyant was removed to the State Insane Asylum at Jacksonville.

Herndon quotes an incident concerning the Wyant case, told by Joseph E. McDonald, a fellow lawyer on the Eighth Circuit, in these words:[1]

[1] Herndon, W. H., *Op. cit.,* p. 278.

Early in 1858 [1857?], at Danville, Illinois, I met Lincoln, Swett, and others who had returned from court in an adjoining county, and were discussing the various features of a murder trial in which Lincoln had made a vigorous fight for the prosecution and Swett had defended. The plea of the defense was insanity. On inquiring the name of the defendant I was surprised to learn that it was my old friend Isaac Wyant, formerly of Indiana. I told them that I had been Wyant's counsel frequently and had defended him from almost every charge in the calendar of crimes; and that he was a weak brother and could be lead into almost everything. At once Lincoln began to manifest great interest in Wyant's history, and had to be told all about him. The next day on the way to the courthouse he told me he had been greatly troubled over what I related about Wyant; that his sleep had been disturbed by the fear that he had been too bitter and unrelenting in his prosecution of him. "I acted," he said "on the theory that he was 'possuming' insanity, and now I fear I have been too severe and that the poor fellow may be insane after all. If he cannot realize the wrong of his crime, then I was wrong in aiding to punish him."

The trial of Wyant was a very exciting one, and the court room was packed during the entire period. What a battle it must have been, headed by Abraham Lincoln and Leonard Swett! Hon. Joseph W. Fifer of Bloomington, later Governor of Illinois was confirmed in his early resolve to become a lawyer when he heard the eloquent plea of Mr. Swett on behalf of Wyant. Mr. Swett became at once prominent in legal circles, and he developed into probably the greatest criminal lawyer of his time. He must indeed have been a giant, to defeat Abraham Lincoln! [1]

XXXIII

A S a diversion from the labors of his law prac-tice, Abraham Lincoln took up lyceum lec-turing. His famous lecture entitled "Discoveries and Inventions" was probably first delivered in Bloomington, at Centre Hall, on April 6, 1858, before a large and interested audience. Miss Ida M. Tarbell [2] states that the first delivery of this lecture was at Beardstown in May, 1858, so the earlier date in Bloomington was apparently the first. Carl Sandburg [3] places the first delivery of the lecture in February, 1860, as does the Edi-tor's note to Henry A. Melvin's published version of the lecture. Lincoln wrote two lectures on the same subject, with only minor differences, the Melvin edition being published in 1909 [4] and the other in a volume entitled *Addresses and Letters of Lincoln* (New York 1904). The lecture opened in this wise: "Man is not the only animal who labors; but he is the only one who *improves* his workmanship. This improvement he effects

[1] References for the Wyant Case may be found in the Blooming-ton *Daily Pantgraph*, April 1-14, 1857, and in McLean Co. Histori-cal Society, *Op. cit.*, vol. ii, p. 342.
[2] Tarbell, I. M., *In the Footsteps of the Lincolns*, p. 345.
[3] Sandburg, Carl, *Op. cit.*, vol. ii, p. 237.
[4] *Sunset*, vol. xxii (1909) 463-74.

by *Discoveries* and *Inventions*. His first important discovery was the fact that he was naked;
and his first invention was the fig-leaf apron. This
simple article—the apron—made of leaves, seems
to have been the origin of clothing—the one thing
for which nearly half of the toil and care of the
human race has ever since been expended." The
lecture was interesting, although read from manuscript, but not generally a financial success, as
witness what happened even in Bloomington a
year later.

XXXIV

THE year 1858 was politically exciting in Illinois, as there was to be an election for Senator in the fall which promised to be closely con-
tested. As the result of a call of the McLean
County Central Committee, the Republicans of
the County assembled in the Court House at
Bloomington on June 5th. The *Daily Pantagraph,* of April 29th, had stated that the Chicago
Tribune gave McLean County the credit for being the first to issue a call for a Republican
County Convention. At this Mass Convention,
Jesse W. Fell offered the following resolution,
among others, which was unanimously adopted: [1]

Resolved, That the Hon. A. Lincoln is our *first, last
and only* choice for the vacancy soon to occur in the United States Senate; (Applause, and shouts, "Don't read

[1] Bloomington *Daily Pantagraph,* June 7, 1858.

any more," "That's enough," etc. Mr. Fell, however, read on, the conclusion being greeted with great applause—Sec.) and that despite all influences at home or abroad, domestic or foreign, the Republicans of Illinois, as with the voice of one man, are unalterably so resolved; to the end, that we may have a *big man,* with a *big mind,* and a *big heart,* to represent our *big State.*

Thus the loyalty of Bloomington for Lincoln was early evidenced. In the issue of June 4th the *Pantagraph* graphically showed the unbroken connection between the Republican Platform adopted at the Bloomington Convention in 1856, the Platform of the National Republican Convention of the same year, and the principles of the Party at the time of writing. The paper added: "We publish this morning the Philadelphia and Bloomington platforms of 1856, which are being so generally reaffirmed by the county meetings throughout the State,—that all may see what the principles of the Republican party were in 1856, and what they are now. The lapse of time has vindicated the wisdom of those principles, and confirmed the faith of those who supported them in the last campaign." Can any other Republican meeting held earlier than the Bloomington Convention of 1856, outside the State of Illinois, show a like continuity?

XXXV

THE Republican State Convention met in Springfield on June 16, 1858, and nominated Abraham Lincoln for United States Senator. Lincoln was called upon to make an address, and he responded with his famous "House Divided" speech which presented to the nation the principle which he had conceived and previously set forth in Bloomington. " 'A house divided against itself cannot stand.' I believe this government cannot endure; permanently half *slave* and half *free*." He had been advised by his friends not to say it, but he was so convinced of its truth he was willing to stand or fall with it. Lincoln's friends were afraid its "delivery would make Abolitionists of all the North and slavery propagandists of all the South, and thereby precipitate a struggle which might end in disunion." [1] Even afterward, Leonard Swett tells us, "in the summer of 1859, when he was dining with a party of his intimate friends at Bloomington, the subject of his Springfield speech was discussed. We all insisted that it was a great mistake; but he justified himself, and finally said, 'Well, gentlemen, you may think that speech was a mistake; but I never have believed it was, and you will see the day when you will consider it was the wisest

[1] Herndon, W. H., *Op. cit.*, p. 325.

thing I ever said.' " [1] Lincoln was right, as succeeding events proved.

An enthusiastic Editorial in the Bloomington *Daily Pantagraph* for June 19th described the Springfield Convention as follows:

The Republican State Convention at Springfield on Wednesday last was all that the most ardent Republican could have desired, in numbers, enthusiasm, devotion to the principles of the party, and readiness to sacrifice mere personal preferences to the sentiment of the majority. . . . We have seen many conventions of many parties, but never before have we seen a delegate convention so large, so enthusiastic, so harmonious, and so well satisfied with its work when its business was done. . . .

By supplementary resolution, our present able State Administration is heartily endorsed, our Senator and Representatives in Congress are properly commended, and Abraham Lincoln is declared to be our *first* and *only* choice for the next vacancy in the Senate.

On this latter point, *unanimity* is a weak word to express the universal and intense feeling of the Convention. Lincoln! *Lincoln!!* LINCOLN!!!—was the cry everywhere, whenever the Senatorship was alluded to. Delegates from Chicago and from Cairo, from the Wabash and the Illinois, from the north, the centre and the south, were alike fired with enthusiasm whenever that loved name was breathed. Enemies at home, and misjudging friends abroad, who have looked for dissension among us on the question of the Senatorship, will please take notice that our nomination is an *unanimous* one, and that in the event of a Republican majority in the next Legislature, no other name than Lincoln's will be mentioned or thought of by a solitary Republican legislator.

[1] Herndon, W. H., *Ibid,* p. 426.

XXXVI

ON the evening of July 9, 1858, Abraham Lincoln heard Stephen A. Douglas open his campaign for the Senatorship in a speech from the balcony of the Tremont House in Chicago. The following evening Lincoln answered Douglas in an address from the same place, and after spending a few days in Chicago he arrived at his home in Springfield on July 15th. The following day, July 16th, Douglas set out on a speaking tour of the State in a private railroad car, with Bloomington as the first stop. Contrary to the statements of Beveridge and Milton, Lincoln was not on this train.[1] Douglas arrived in Bloomington at 3:30 in the afternoon, and Lincoln arrived from Springfield at six o'clock. The Bloomington *Pantagraph* gave the following colorful account of the arrival of Douglas and of his speech in the evening:[2]

Hon. Stephen A. Douglas arrived in this city at half past three o'clock yesterday afternoon. The train on which he arrived was tastefully decorated with flags and on each side of the baggage car were the words "S. A. Douglas, the Champion of Popular Sovereignty." About

[1] Beveridge, A. J., *Op. cit.*, vol. ii, p. 610.
Milton, G. F., *The Eve of Conflict* (Boston 1934) p. 321.
Cf. Angle, P. M., *Op. cit.*, p. 237.
[2] Bloomington *Daily Pantagraph*, July 17, 1858; also quoted in part in *The Lincoln-Douglas Debates of 1858,* ed. by E. E. Sparks. Illinois State Historical Library, Collections, vol. iii (Springfield, Ill. 1908) p. 50-51.

a thousand persons—more than one half of whom were Republicans—witnessed Judge D's arrival. Just before the cars reached the depot Pullen's Brass Band commenced playing "Hail Columbia" and when the cars stopped, the Bloomington Guards commenced firing a national salute of thirty-two guns. Judge Douglas was in the hind-most passenger car—an open car, upon which was placed a brass six-pounder, bringing up the rear. . . .

At seven o'clock in the evening the Court-house bell rang,—and Judge Douglas, escorted by the Guards, and the brass band, and a goodly number of Democrats, proceeded to the public square. . . .

The Judge commenced speaking at half past seven, and concluded at a quarter before ten. His speech did not differ materially from the one made by him in Chicago on the evening of the ninth instant. . . .

He spoke to an audience of about two thousand persons. His Democratic listeners were highly pleased with his speech. They viewed it as a masterly effort—and we are willing to admit that the Judge did, on the whole, make a very good speech in a very bad cause.

During the latter part of his speech he referred to one of the positions assumed by Hon. Abraham Lincoln in his late speech at Springfield. We thought some of his remarks in reference to Mr. Lincoln were not much calculated to advance his (Judge D's) political interests. . . .

As soon as Judge Douglas retired, loud calls were made for Hon. Abraham Lincoln. Mr. L. held back for a little while, but the crowd finally succeeded in inducing him to come upon the stand. He was received with three rousing cheers—much louder than those given to Judge Douglas. He remarked that he appeared before the audience for the purpose of saying that he would take an early opportunity to give his views to the citizens of this place regarding the matters spoken of in Judge Douglas' speech. "This meeting," said Mr. Lincoln, "was called by the friends of Judge Douglas, and it would be improper for me to address it." Mr. L. then retired, amid loud cheering.

Lincoln's arrival in Bloomington on this occasion is told by Leonard W. Volk, the famous sculptor who made the life-mask of Lincoln and casts of his hands: [1]

My first meeting with Abraham Lincoln was in 1858, when the celebrated senatorial contest opened in Chicago between him and Stephen A. Douglas. I was invited by the latter to accompany him and his party by a special train to Springfield, to which train was attached a platform-car having on board a cannon, which made considerable noise on the journey. At Bloomington we all stopped over night as Douglas had a speech to make there in the evening. The party went to the Landon House, the only hotel, I believe, in the place at the time.

While we were sitting in the hotel office after supper, Mr. Lincoln entered, carrying an old carpet-bag in his hand, and wearing a weather-beaten silk hat,—too large, apparently, for his head,—a long, loosely fitting frock-coat, of black alpaca, and vest and trousers of the same material. He walked up to the counter, and saluting the clerk pleasantly, passed the bag over to him, and inquired if he was too late for supper. The clerk replied that supper was over, but thought enough could be "scraped up" for him.

"All right," said Mr. Lincoln, "I don't want much."

[1] Volk, L. W., "The Lincoln Life-Mask and How it was Made" in *Century Magazine,* vol. xxiii (1881-82) 223; reprinted in Whitney, H. C., *Life on the Circuit with Lincoln* (Boston 1892) p. 539-40; and in Illinois State Historical Soc., *Journal,* vol. viii (1915-16) p. 238.

Meanwhile, he said he would wash the dust off ; he was certainly very dusty, for it was the month of June [July] and quite warm. While he was so engaged several old friends, who had learned of his arrival, rushed in to see him, some of them shouting out, "How are you, Old Abe?" Mr. Lincoln grasped them by the hand in his cordial manner, with the broadest and pleasantest smile on his rugged face.

The following morning at 3 :30 o'clock Lincoln was a passenger on the Douglas train as it pulled out of Bloomington for Springfield.

XXXVII

ON July 24, 1858, while in Chicago, Abraham Lincoln challenged Stephen A. Douglas, who was also in Chicago, to a series of debates in the State of Illinois on the issues of the day. On the 30th following Douglas accepted, and set forth a schedule of seven debates for Lincoln's approval, to which the latter agreed although Douglas arranged it for his own benefit. The first debate took place at Ottawa on August 21st, which was followed by the Freeport debate on the 27th, during which Lincoln said the Republican Party was founded at Bloomington. The remaining schedule was Sept. 15th, Jonesboro; Sept. 18th, Charleston; Oct. 7th, Galesburg; Oct. 13th, Quincy; and Oct. 15th, Alton. In his opening speech at Quincy, Lincoln elaborated upon what he had said at Freeport regarding the Republican Party, in these words: [1]

> In the month of May, 1856, the elements in the State of Illinois which have since consolidated into the Republican party assembled together in a State convention at Bloomington. They adopted at that time what, in political language, is called a platform. In June of the same year, the elements of the Republican party in the nation assembled together in a national convention at Philadelphia. They adopted what is called the national platform. In June, 1858,—the present year,—the Republicans of Illinois reassembled at Springfield in State Convention, and adopted again their platform, as I suppose, not differing in any essential particular from either of the former ones, but perhaps adding something in relation to the new developments of political progress in the country.

Thus is the continuity from the Bloomington Republican Convention again illustrated! The debates with Douglas, conceived first by Jesse W. Fell of Bloomington, thus carried out and with Lincoln the conceded victor, made Lincoln for the first time a nationally known figure. Until nationally known, his rise to the presidency was impossible.

XXXVIII

ON Saturday, September 4, 1858, Bloomington gave a big demonstration in honor of her idol—Abraham Lincoln. Early in the afternoon

[1] Lincoln, Abraham, *Complete Works,* vol. iv, p. 311-12.

a long procession marched from the Court House Square to the residence of Judge David Davis, there received Lincoln and escorted him down Washington street to the Square. There were banners flying bearing such mottoes as "Our country, our whole country and nothing but our country;" "The Union—it must be preserved;" "Freedom is National—Slavery is Sectional." Above the north door of the Court House was the representation of a ship in a storm, and underneath were the words: "Don't give up the ship—give her a new pilot." On the north and west sides of the Court House were streamers, which indicated that McLean county was "for Abram Lincoln—first, last and forever." The Square was packed with people; Leonard Swett made the reception speech. Lincoln replied with a two-hour address on the slavery agitation, saying in part: [1]

It is not merely an agitation got up to help men into office. . . . The same cause has rent asunder the great Methodist and Presbyterian churches, and is now disturbing the Tract Society. . . .

It will not cease until a crisis has been reached and passed. When the public mind rests in the belief that the evil is in a course of ultimate extinction, it will become quiet. We have no right to interfere with slavery in the States. We only want to restrict it to where it is. We have never had an agitation except when it was endeavored to spread it. . . . The framers of the Constitution prohibited slavery (not *in* the Constitution, but the *same men* did it) north of the Ohio River where it did

[1] Bloomington *Daily Pantagraph*, Sept. 6, 1858.

not exist, and did not prohibit it south of that River
where it *did* exist. . . . I fight it in its *advancing* phase,
and wish to place it in the same attitude that the framers
of the government did. . . . There is no moral argument
that can be made for carrying slaves into new territory,
which will not also stand good in favor of the African
slave trade.

Former Governor of Illinois, Joseph W.
Fifer, in a public address which he delivered in
Bloomington on December 4, 1935, after he had
passed his ninety-fifth birthday, described the occasion of this speech at which he was present. He
spoke as follows: [1]

I heard him [Lincoln] make his greatest speech in
September, 1858, the year of the joint debates. There
were none of these here. Douglas and Lincoln often made
speeches in different places between the debates. George
B. McClellan, then the engineer of the Illinois Central
road, brought Douglas to Bloomington to speak [on
July 16th]. Both [Adlai E.] Stevenson and [James S.]
Ewing said it was the greatest speech Douglas ever
made. This was a strong Republican locality. Judge
David Davis, Jesse Fell and Hudson Burr, alarmed at
the effect of the Douglas speech, wrote to Lincoln to
come and answer it. This he did in the middle [the 4th]
of September, 1858.

The speech was given in the Old Court House yard—
the courthouse was a four wall building, not much larger
than a good big dry goods box, on the south side of the
court house yard. The sides and the rear were roped out
to the street on the north. Lincoln took dinner with
Judge Davis and a few friends who had been invited.

There were no seats. All had to stand. Three times

[1] Bloomington *Daily Pantagraph*, Dec. 5, 1935.

as many can be put in the same space standing. Two carriages drove up to the west side. Lincoln with Davis and his son were in one. I saw them get out. There was a fine stand for the speakers. Lincoln, like Saul of Tarsus, seemed to tower over Leonard Swett on his right, and David Davis to the left. My older brother, later killed in the Civil war, had read how Lincoln had collected paper and bark to make light by which to read law, and this applied to us. As boys will, we got into the crowd and elbowed our way to be in front of Lincoln. We were only 10 or 15 feet from him.

Davis called for order and introduced Swett, who made an eloquent speech, a beautiful speech of introduction. Lincoln got up. I thought he never would get through getting up; he undoubled and stood away above the others. He wore a black suit. He didn't seem awkward to me. He handled himself well. His first sentence didn't seem to suit him, and he came back to try it again. It made a slow start, and my brother whispered, "Swett is the better speaker; maybe he'd be a better President."

Soon Lincoln warmed up. My brother whispered later, "Joe, look at those faces!" Every one had faces up to Lincoln with their attention riveted on him. They looked as though they were hewn out of rock. They were sober and serious, and seemed to feel that some great calamity was impending.

Douglas had claimed that Lincoln was in favor of negro equality. Lincoln said, "I never have been in favor of negro equality. I don't believe in it. They are not equal in color, education and social attainments." He raised his arm, with fist clenched, declaring emphatically there was no reason why a man who wished to give a negro woman her rights should also wish to make her his wife. "But in the right to eat bread his own hand has earned the negro is the equal of Judge Douglas or myself."

This was Lincoln's political position, as it was that of the Republican Party, and from the day of his Bloomington Convention speech he never lost sight of the moral evil of the institution of slavery. The demonstration continued into the evening, with speeches by several men, and Bloomington was unqualifiedly for Lincoln.

XXXIX

FROM the fifth of October, 1857, until June, 1860, Major's Hall was occupied by the Illinois State Normal University, while its own building was under construction, and thus Bloomington was without a large public hall. Early in September, 1858, Dr. C. Wakefield started the construction of a large hall in the third and fourth floors of his building in Phœnix Block, to seat 1200 people. It was known at first as Phœnix Hall, then for a short time as Liberty Hall, but the former name was permanently adopted. The Hall was completed and dedicated by an enthusiastic Republican meeting on October 22, 1858. Leonard Swett, recently convalescent from an illness, made a speech of two hours, often interrupted by great applause from the packed house. The *Pantagraph,* the following day, stated "he followed Mr. Douglas through his maze of perversions and misrepresentations, and refuted his calumnies in an admirable manner." Pullen's brass band attended, and opened and closed the meeting with music. Thereafter Phœnix Hall became Republican Headquarters for McLean County, not only during Lincoln's campaigns but during Grant's and Hayes' presidential campaigns. It was also the scene of many lectures by prominent men, such as Horace Greeley on "Great Men," December 22, 1858, and Bayard Taylor on "Life in the North," May 13, 1859. The Hall had still another use, as we shall see presently.

XL

ON November 2, 1858, came the anxiously awaited election day for State offices. Lincoln received a popular majority vote of 4,085 over Douglas for U. S. Senator, but not enough legislative votes to send him to Washington. However, Bloomington and McLean County loyally stood by Lincoln, as is evidenced by the *Pantagraph* the next morning:

WHOLE REPUBLICAN TICKET ELECTED!

600 MAJORITY FOR SWETT!

HURRAH FOR LINCOLN!

The battle is over, and so far as McLean county at least is concerned, we have again to congratulate our friends on a glorious Republican victory.

THIS TABLET
MARKS THE SITE OF
OLD LIBERTY HALL
LATER
PHOENIX HALL
WHERE
ABRAHAM LINCOLN
MADE A NUMBER OF SPEECHES

PLACED 1924 BY
HARRIET WAKEFIELD BRADY
A MEMBER OF
LETITIA GREEN STEVENSON CHAPTER
DAUGHTERS OF THE AMERICAN REVOLUTION
IN MEMORY OF HER FATHER
DR. C. WAKEFIELD
A FRIEND OF ABRAHAM LINCOLN
AND OWNER OF PHOENIX HALL

Upper right—Major's Hall in 1856. *Upper left*—Tablet marking site of Phoenix Hall.
Lower—Phoenix Block as it appeared in 1858-1860.

We have been up all night receiving returns and rejoicing with our brethren. The boastful anticipations of the Democracy are all proved wrong, and McLean county stands erect, as a staunch and reliable Republican county. She has repudiated Douglas, and nobly endorsed the gallant Lincoln. McLean county for ever!

Leonard Swett was elected to the Legislature, and on January 5, 1859, he voted for Lincoln for Senator, but Douglas was elected by a vote of 54 to 41.

XLI

A STORY which admirably illustrates Lincoln's ready wit about this time is told by Mr. John H. Wickizer, of Bloomington, as follows: [1] "In 1858, in the court at Bloomington, Mr. Lincoln was engaged in a case of no great importance; but the attorney on the other side, Mr. S——, [John M. Scott?] a young lawyer of fine abilities (now a judge of the Supreme Court of the State), was always very sensitive about being beaten, and in this case manifested unusual zeal and interest. The case lasted until late at night, when it was finally submitted to the jury. Mr. S—— spent a sleepless night in anxiety, and early next morning learned, to his great chagrin, that he had lost the case. Mr. Lincoln met him at the Court House, and asked him what had become of his case. With lugubrious countenance and

[1] Lamon, W. H., *Op. cit.,* p. 325.

melancholy tone, Mr. S—— said, 'It's gone to hell.'—'Oh, well!' replied Lincoln, 'then you'll see it again!'"

XLII

JESSE W. FELL, of Bloomington, was not only the first man to suggest the Lincoln-Douglas Debates, as has been stated, but he was also the first man seriously to think of Lincoln as a presidential possibility and to urge Lincoln to become a candidate. As in the former case, we are very fortunate to have Mr. Fell's own account of the circumstances of this important proposal, written in March, 1872, and I herewith present it in full: [1]

In the fall of 1858, during the discussion between Senator Douglas and Mr. Lincoln, I had occasion to visit the Middle and Eastern States; and as the whole country was then agitated by the slavery question, and that discussion cut a prominent figure in the agitation, I was frequently applied to for information in reference to Mr. Lincoln. I felt my State pride flattered by these inquiries, and still more to find the *New York Tribune,* and other papers, publishing copious extracts from these discussions, taken from the Chicago press. I did what little I could to satisfy so laudable a curiosity, not thinking, at first, that anything further would come of this discus-

[1] Published by the Misses Alice and Fannie Fell. Also in Oldroyd, O. H., ed., *The Lincoln Memorial: Album—Immortelles,* p. 472-77.

sion, in reference to Mr. Lincoln, than his election to the Senate. At length, from the frequency of these inquiries and public notices of the Illinois contest, an impression began to form, that by judicious efforts he could be made the Republican candidate for the presidency in 1860. Very soon after my return home, and after the senatorial contest had closed, one evening, as I passed on the south side of the public square of this city, I espied the tall form of Mr. Lincoln emerging from the court-house door, Judge Davis's court then being in session. I stopped until he came across the street, when, after the usual salutations, I asked him to go with me into my brother's (K. H. Fell) law-office, then kept over what is now the Home Bank. There we sat down, and in the calm twilight of the evening, had substantially the following conversation:—

Fell.—"Lincoln, I have been East, as far as Boston, and up into New Hampshire, traveling in all the New England States, save Maine; in New York, New Jersey, Pennsylvania, Ohio, Michigan and Indiana; and everywhere I hear you talked about. Very frequently I have been asked: 'Who is this man Lincoln, of your State, now canvassing in opposition to Senator Douglas?' Being, as you know, an ardent Republican and your friend, I usually told them we had in Illinois *two* giants instead of one; that Douglas was the little one, as they all knew, but that you were the big one, which they didn't all know. But, seriously, Lincoln, Judge Douglas being so widely known, you are getting a national reputation *through him*, as the result of the late discussion; your speeches, in whole or in part, on both sides, have been pretty extensively published in the East; you are there regarded by discriminating minds as quite a match for him in debate, and the truth is, I have a decided impression that if your popular history and efforts on the slavery question can be sufficiently brought before the people, you can be made a formidable, if not a successful, candidate for the presidency."

Lincoln.—"Oh, Fell, what's the use talking of me for the presidency, whilst we have such men as Seward, Chase and others, who are so much better known to the people, and whose names are so intimately associated with the principles of the Republican party. Everybody knows them; nobody, scarcely, outside of Illinois, knows me. Besides, is it not, as a matter of justice, due to such men, who have carried this movement forward to its present status, in spite of fearful opposition, personal abuse, and hard names? I really think so."

Fell.—"There is much truth in what you say. The men you allude to, occupying more prominent positions, have undoubtedly rendered a larger service in the Republican cause than you have; but the truth is, they have rendered *too much* service to be available candidates. Placing it on the grounds of personal services, or merit, if you please, I concede at once the superiority of their claims. Personal services and merit, however, when incompatible with the public good, must be laid aside. Seward and Chase have both made long records on the slavery question, and have said some very radical things which, however just and true in themselves, and however much these men may challenge our admiration for their courage and devotion to unpopular truths, would seriously damage them in the contest, if nominated. We must bear in mind, Lincoln, that we are yet in a minority; we are struggling against fearful odds for supremacy. We were defeated on this same issue in 1856, and will be again in 1860, unless we get a great many new votes from what may be called the old conservative parties. These will be repelled by the radical utterances and votes of such men as Seward and Chase. What the Republican party wants, to insure success in 1860, is a man of popular origin, of acknowledged ability, committed against slavery aggressions, who has no record to defend and no radicalism of an offensive character to repel votes from parties hitherto adverse. Your discussion with Judge Douglas has demonstrated your ability and your devotion to freedom; you have no embarrassing record; you have sprung from the humble walks of life, sharing in its toils and trials; and if we can only get these facts sufficiently before the people, depend upon it, there is some chance for you. And now, Mr. Lincoln, I come to the *business p*art of this interview. My native State, Pennsylvania, will have a large number of votes to cast for somebody on the question we have been discussing. Pennsylvania doesn't like, over much, New York and her politicians. She has a candidate, Cameron, of her own; but he will not be acceptable to a large number of her own people, much less abroad, and will be dropped. Through an eminent jurist and essayist of my native county in Pennsylvania, favorably known throughout the State, I want to get up a well-considered, well-written newspaper article telling the people who you are and what you have done, that it may be circulated, not only in that State, but elsewhere, and thus help in manufacturing sentiment in your favor. I know your public life, and can furnish items that your modesty would forbid, but I don't know much about your private history: when you were born, and where, the names and origin of your parents, what you did in early life, what your opportunities for education were, etc., and I want you to give me these. Won't you do it?"

Lincoln.—"Fell, I admit the force of much that you say, and admit that I am ambitious, and would like to be President. I am not insensible to the compliment you pay me, and the interest you manifest in the matter; but *there is no such good luck in store for me as the presidency of these United States;* besides, there is nothing in my early history that would interest you or anybody else; and, as Judge Davis says, '*It won't pay.*' Good night."

And thus ended, for the time being, my pet scheme of helping to make Lincoln President. I notified him, however, as his giant form, wrapped in a dilapidated shawl, disappeared in the darkness, that this was not the last of it; that the *facts* must come. The next year, 1859, I was engaged much of the time as the corresponding secretary of the Republican State Central Committee, in traveling over the State and in carrying out plans for a more thorough organization of the Republican party, preparatory to the great contest of 1860. I visited personally a large majority of the counties in the State, and nearly everywhere had the satisfaction of learning that, though many doubted the possibility of nominating Lincoln, most generally it was approved of. This fact became in time very apparent to Lincoln himself, whom I not infrequently met in my travels; and in the month of December of that year, feeling that perhaps it *would* "pay", I induced him to place in my hands this eminently characteristic paper.

The paper referred to was the only autobiography Lincoln wrote before his nomination, the text of which is here presented.[1] Its value

[1] See Appendix II. Paul M. Angle (Abraham Lincoln Association, *Bulletin,* no. xxviii, 1932, p. 10) speaks of the erection of a tablet in front of the Bloomington Court House marking the site of the writing of Lincoln's Autobiography, and he asks for the authority which cites Bloomington rather than Springfield for the place of writing. The best authority whom I know for the Bloomington claim is Judge Lawrence Weldon (McLean Co. Historical Society, *Op. cit.,* vol. i, p. 349), who was certainly in a position to know. The same claim is made by Rexford Newcomb in his *In the Lincoln Country* (Philadelphia 1928) p. 148. It is impossible to set an exact date for the writing of the Autobiography, wherever written, but it is not unlikely that Lincoln was in Bloomington attending Court on December 16, 17, 18, 1859. He would have been urged repeatedly by

cannot be overestimated. After many repeated requests by Mr. Fell, Lincoln sent the autobiography with the following characteristic letter: [1]

SPRINGFIELD, *Dec. 20, 1859.*

J. W. FELL, ESQ.

My dear Sir:

Herewith is a little sketch, as you requested. There is not much of it, for the reason, I suppose, that there is not much of me. If anything be made out of it, I wish it to be modest, and not to go beyond the materials. If it was thought necessary to incorporate anything from any

Jesse W. Fell to write the Autobiography, and perhaps on the 18th sat at a desk in the Court House and wrote it. He probably wanted to think it over further before giving it to Mr. Fell and took it with him to Springfield, from where he mailed it to Mr. Fell on the 20th. The date given on the tablet for the writing of the Autobiography, "during the winter of 1858-59," assumes that Lincoln wrote it shortly after Mr. Fell first requested it of him, an assumption which has no basis in fact so far as I know. On the contrary, Lincoln's statement of his life was not sent to Mr. Fell until December 20, 1859, or during the winter of 1859-60, and it seems more likely that he wrote it shortly before the latter date. The tablet calls it "the only autobiography of his early life," forgetting that Lincoln wrote a longer autobiography for John Locke Scripps of the Chicago *Press and Tribune* after his nomination for the presidency.

William E. Barton, in his *President Lincoln* (2 vols., Indianapolis 1933), devotes a chapter to this first autobiography of Lincoln's. In a footnote devoted to a discussion of the date on which Mr. Fell first suggested to Lincoln that he write the autobiography, he states that "the only known visit of Lincoln to Bloomington in 1858 after the close of the Lincoln-Douglas debates was Thursday, December 30." We know, however, that Lincoln was in Bloomington on December 21st as the guest of Judge David Davis, and wrote in the autograph album of young George P. Davis. As a matter of fact, Lincoln's whereabouts are not definitely accounted for on December 20, 22-24, but as court was in session in Bloomington at that time there is every reason to believe that he was there attending to business. The conversation between Lincoln and Mr. Fell, therefore, could have taken place on any day between December 20th and the 24th, as well as on the 30th.

[1] Oldroyd, O. H., ed., *Op. cit.,* p. 477.

of my speeches, I suppose there would be no objections. Of course, it must not appear to have been written by myself.

Yours very truly,

A. LINCOLN.

Mr. Fell continued his account as follows:

I made some additions to the facts, therein contained, bearing upon his political history, and immediately for- warded them to the Hon. Joseph J. Lewis, of Westches- ter, Pennsylvania, since Commissioner of Internal Rev- enue. These constituted the basis on which that gentleman wrote a biographical sketch and notice of his public ser- vices, altogether the most complete and reliable, that ever appeared prior to his nomination. It had a wide circulation, not only in Pennsylvania, but in Illinois and throughout the country. As an evidence of its superior merit, this same gentleman, who was one of the leading delegates at Chicago from Pennsylvania, remarked to me, the morning after the nomination, that the Chicago press had complimented him very handsomely, by repro- ducing his article almost entire, in response to the in- quiry, then become general, "Who is Abraham Lincoln?"

Thus was Abraham Lincoln launched as a presidential candidate. Meanwhile Mr. Fell had convinced David Davis and Leonard Swett of the feasibility of making Lincoln President, and Lincoln found himself backed by as loyal and ef- ficient a triumvirate as he could well have.

XLIII

O N the evening of April 8, 1859, Abraham
Lincoln was scheduled to deliver his lecture
on "Discoveries and Inventions" in Phœnix Hall
for the benefit of the Ladies' Library Association. The lecture had been announced in the papers a few days previously, and the tickets had
been on sale for twenty-five cents each. The *Pantagraph* reported the event as follows: [1]

The lecture by Hon. A. Lincoln on the subject of Inventions, advertised to be given in Phoenix Hall last
night for the benefit of the Ladies' Library Association,
did not come off. Either from a want of sufficiently general notice, or from the fact of the same discourse as we
suppose having been once delivered in our city already,
(last winter,) the audience which attended in Phoenix
Hall was not so large as it should have been, and it was
concluded to adjourn the matter. We regret this greatly, for we are very sure that the lecture would have re-
paid the biggest audience that ever got into Phoenix
Hall.

Mr. John H. Burnham of Bloomington, one
of the founders of the Illinois State Historical
Society, wrote a letter to his father in Massachu-
setts on May 19, 1860, the day after Lincoln's
nomination for the presidency. In this letter he

[1] Bloomington *Daily Pantagraph,* Apr. 9, 1859. *The Weekly
Pantagraph* of Apr. 13th reprinted the account without change of
"last night."

tells in these words of attending Phœnix Hall on
this occasion to hear Lincoln speak: [1]

> I have seen Lincoln several times, and heard him speak
> once. His popularity as a speaker consists in joking and
> story telling, and I have heard many better orators. I
> heard him one year ago on a law case. In the evening
> he was advertised to lecture on *Invention*, for the benefit
> of the Ladies Library Association, admittance 25cts.
>
> I paid a quarter and went early to get a seat. It was
> a beautiful evening, and the lecture had been well ad-
> vertised but for some reason not yet explained, only
> about 40 persons were present, and old Abe would not
> speak to such a small crowd, and they paid us back our
> quarters at the door.

Thus in the town in Illinois which was most
friendly to him, was Lincoln's lyceum lecturing
finally a failure.

XLIV

ALTHOUGH Lincoln was a resident of
Springfield his best friends were in Bloomington, and he went there on every possible occasion. He rarely put up in a hotel while in town,
but generally was entertained by Fell, Davis,
Wakefield or other friends. He made the law office of Kersey Fell, over the Home Bank in Phœnix Block, his headquarters, and there his friends
would congregate and discuss with him the cur-

[1] Burnham, J. H. in Pratt, H. E., "When Lincoln Failed to
Draw a Crowd" in Ill. State Historical Soc., *Journal*, vol. xxviii
(1935-36) p. 95-97.

rent problems of politics and religion. He seldom talked on the subject of religion in public, but when alone with these friends he talked freely. His radical views on the subject were well known to them—agreeable to most of them—and they felt the need of a liberal religious organization. There was a Universalist church in town, founded in 1851, to which the Wakefield family and other friends belonged, but this was not radical enough for them. Accordingly on the evening of July 10, 1859, there gathered in Kersey Fell's office about twenty of Lincoln's friends to consider the advisability of founding a new society suitable to their views. Among them were the Fells, the Wakefields, and Charles P. Merriman, Editor of the *Pantagraph* and former Mayor of Bloomington. Mr. Jesse W. Fell was appointed Secretary and authorized to write Rev. Charles G. Ames of Somerville, Mass., an unattached minister whom a younger brother of Mr. Fell had met, to ask if he would come and preach for a month as an experiment. Mr. Ames accepted the invitation and preached for the first time on July 24th at Phœnix Hall, which had been donated for the purpose by Dr. Wakefield. The experiment was successful, and on August 8th the Free Congregational Society was organized with thirty-two members. Mr. Ames was the minister until 1862, and Ichabod Codding, the abolitionist, was minister in 1865. The Society met in Phœnix Hall regularly until 1868, when a church building was completed, and in 1885 the Society became the Unitarian Church of Bloomington which it is today. Later Mr. Ames became a famous Unitarian minister in Boston.[1] Among the members of this liberal religious society were nearly all the Republican leaders and newspaper men in Bloomington, and they did valiant service for Lincoln in his later campaigns. If any church can claim Abraham Lincoln it is the Unitarian Church in Bloomington.

XLV

THE biographical sketch of Lincoln written by Mr. Joseph J. Lewis of Westchester, Pa., from material supplied him by Lincoln himself and Jesse W. Fell, was printed in the *Chester County* (Pa.) *Times* on February 11, 1860, and reprinted in the Bloomington *Weekly Pantagraph* for February 22, 1860. A short quotation from it may be of interest here:[2]

[1] Prince, E. M., *The Unitarian Church of Bloomington, Ill.* (Bloomington 1909).

Wakefield, Homer, and Ames, C. G. in *Christian Register,* vol. lxxxviii (1909) 233, 286-88, 342-43.

Morehouse, F. M. I., *Op. cit.,* p. 92-95.

[2] For further details of the use made of Lincoln's Autobiography, see Fell, J. W. in Lamon, W. H., *Op. cit.,* Appendix; also in Lamon's *Recollections of Abraham Lincoln, 1847-1865,* ed. by D. L. Teillard (2nd ed. Washington 1911) p. 11-12. The complete text of the Lewis biography is reprinted in Barton, W. E., "The Lincoln of the Biographers" in Illinois State Historical Soc., *Transactions,* vol. xxxvi (1929) p. 81-86. Barton makes the claim that it "has not hitherto been known" that Lincoln had any part in the compilation of the Lewis biography, (p. 63), but since Mr. Fell wrote two

He [Lincoln] fully appreciated the importance of the slavery issue [from 1849 to 1854], and felt the force of the moral causes that must influence the question, and he never failed to appeal to the moral sentiment of the people in aid of the argument drawn from political sources, and to illuminate his theme with the lofty inspirations of an eloquence, pleading for the rights of humanity. . . .

From his thorough conviction of the growing magnitude of the slave question and of the need of a strong effort to preserve the territories to freedom, Mr. Lincoln was among the first to join in the formation of the Republican party, although the public opinion around him [in Springfield] was strongly adverse to that movement. He exerted himself for the organization of the Republican forces in Illinois, and attended the first Republican Convention held in the State. This was in Bloomington in May, 1856. His speech in that convention was of surprising power and eloquence, and produced great effect.

An Editorial in the same issue of the *Pantagraph* ran as follows:

That Mr. Lincoln is the choice of the Republicans of Illinois for the Presidency at the Chicago Convention, there can be no doubt; and there can be but little doubt that he will be the choice of the Northwest. . . . With all due respect to the claims of others, to their preferences and opinions, we most earnestly commend Mr. Lincoln

accounts in which Lincoln's part was described, which were published in the Lamon biography (1872) and in Oldroyd's *Lincoln Memorial* (1883) respectively, the claim is spurious. The Lewis biography was the first published "Life" of Lincoln, and was the source of Horace Greeley's Editorial sketch in the *New York Tribune* of May 19, 1860, and of the similar sketch by John Locke Scripps in the *Chicago Press and Tribune* of the same date, as well as the next three campaign biographies.

to the attention of his Republican friends throughout the Union as a most worthy and available candidate for the Presidency in the campaign which is soon to open.

Thereafter, each Editorial column of the *Pantagraph* was headed by these words: "For President, Hon. Abraham Lincoln, of Illinois, Subject to the National Convention at Chicago, May 16th. For Governor, Hon. Leonard Swett, of McLean, Subject to the State Convention at Decatur, May 9th." The campaign of 1860 was already under way.

XLVI

THE year 1860 was the busiest and most exciting in the life of Lincoln up to that time, starting with his famous Cooper Union speech in New York on February 27th. Bloomington was early in pushing Lincoln for the presidency, on March 17th, by organizing a Lincoln Club. The *Weekly Pantagraph,* of the 21st, gave the following account:

At a meeting of the Republicans of Bloomington, on Saturday night last, at the Court House, a Lincoln Club was formed for the purpose of eliciting and circulating liberal political sentiments upon the exciting questions now agitating the public mind, and to labor by all fair and honorable means, to influence the voters of this section of the country to cast their ballots in the approaching Presidential election in favor of the Republican candidate for President of the United States, and for the candidates of the same party for the subordinate offices, in the political campaign of 1860.

The club organized by adopting a Constitution and By Laws; and electing the following officers:

DR. WM. C. HOBBS, *President*
DR. E. THOMAS,
DR. McCANN DUNN, } *V. Presidents.*
C. P. MERRIMAN, *Secretary.*
WM. H. HANNA,
J. H. WICKIZER,
HARVEY HOGG, } *Committee of Managers*
T. F. MITCHELL,
JAMES O'DONNELL,
C. P. MERRIMAN,
W. W. ORME, } *Corresponding Secretaries.*
HUDSON BURR

It is remarkable that this Republican organization should be called the Lincoln Club, as Lincoln was not yet chosen the State Republican candidate for President, and so it illustrates again how strongly Bloomington was for Lincoln.

XLVII

ON April 2, 1860, a McLean County Republican Mass Meeting was held at the Court House in Bloomington for the purpose of appointing twelve delegates from the County to the State Republican Convention to be held at Decatur on May 9th. The *Daily Pantagraph,* the next day, remarked:

During the absence of the nominating committee, Harvey Hogg, Esq., with a few appropriate prefatory remarks, introduced the following resolutions:

Resolved, That we, the Republicans of McLean Co., are thoroughly impressed with the conviction that the Hon. Abraham Lincoln, above all others, mentioned in connection with the Republican nomination for the Presidency is the available candidate for that position; and that the spotless purity and integrity of his character and his eminent abilities mark him as the man peculiarly fitted to restore the government to the policy of our fathers; and, therefore, under his leadership, we feel that we can march forward to certain victory in behalf of the great principles and the policy of our party.

Resolved, That the Delegates from this County to the Decatur Convention are hereby instructed to vote for, and use all honorable means to secure the nomination of our distinguished fellow citizen, Hon. Leonard Swett, for the office of Governor.

The resolutions were unanimously adopted.

Thus Bloomington wanted Lincoln to be the State Republican candidate for the Presidency, regardless of the wishes of other parts of the State.

XLVIII

TUESDAY, April 10, 1860, was the occasion of a political speech by Abraham Lincoln in Phœnix Hall. The meeting was reported by the Bloomington *Daily Pantagraph* the next day as follows:

Notwithstanding the rain and the mud, last night, Phoenix Hall was full to its capacity of attentive listeners to the speech of Mr. Lincoln. . . . The remarks were characteristic—clear, appropriate, forcible and conclusive on every point made. Mr. Lincoln is probably the fairest and most honest political speaker in the country. While he convinces the understanding by arriving at legitimate and unavoidable sequences, he wins the hearts of his hearers by the utmost fairness and good humor. Several of his home thrusts, last night, went through the sophisms and duplicities of the Shamocracy with a terribly damaging effect.

XLIX

THE Illinois State Republican Convention was held at Decatur on May 9, 1860. The delegates who came, otherwise than from McLean County, were by no means unanimous for Lincoln—some were for William H. Seward, the New York aspirant, and others were for Edward Bates, of St. Louis. But Lincoln's cousin, John Hanks, appeared with two fence rails which bore the inscription that they were "from a lot of 3,000 made in 1830 by Thos. Hanks and Abe Lincoln —whose father was the first pioneer of Macon County." Lincoln was hailed as "The Rail Candidate for President in 1860." After Lincoln had made a speech which had been enthusiastically called for, the following resolution was unanimously adopted:

Resolved, That Abraham Lincoln is the choice of the Republican party of Illinois for the Presidency, and the delegates from this State are instructed to use all honorable means to secure his nomination by the Chicago Convention, and to vote as a unit for him.

Therefore, just a week before the National Republican Convention, Abraham Lincoln was definitely chosen by the State of Illinois as her candidate for the Presidency. Judge David Davis, of Bloomington, was elected one of the delegates at large to the Chicago convention.

L

THE Second National Republican Convention met on Wednesday, May 16, 1860, at Chicago, in a specially erected building called the *Wigwam*. More than a week previously the Illinois delegation, headed by David Davis, and ably assisted by Leonard Swett, opened "Lincoln Headquarters" in the Tremont House. These men worked like demons, and no stone was left unturned to increase Lincoln's chances for the nomination. Leonard Swett, many years later, described the part played by David Davis and the Illinois delegation in the following words: [1]

Judge Davis' political record resolves itself into his work at the Chicago convention, at which Mr. Lincoln

[1] Swett, Leonard, in Ill. State Bar Association, *Op. cit.*, vol. x 1887) p. 79; repr. in *Chicago Legal News*, vol. xix (1886-87) 206-07.

was nominated, and a term of six years in the United States Senate. He had a desire to go to the Chicago convention as a delegate. This came of his friendship for Mr. Lincoln and his own consciousness of strength. He wanted Abraham Lincoln nominated, and he, unconsciously to himself, realized if he could go there as a delegate, he could do more to secure this result than any living man; and so it was an open secret among his friends, before the Decatur convention of 1860, that the judge then wanted to hold the first purely political office of his life. He was consequently elected a delegate-at-large for the State.

He was first on the ground, having, as I remember, gone to Chicago, Friday, a week before Mr. Lincoln was nominated, the following Friday. He found when he got there that no headquarters had been engaged for the Illinois delegation. He sent for John B. Drake, then proprietor of the Tremont house, and the result was an arrangement by which the judge paid a bonus for the evacuation of certain rooms by private families, and these were soon properly marked as the "Illinois Headquarters." Here, without anybody electing him to the position, he at once became the leader of all the Illinois men. He told me when I arrived there Monday to join his staff and go to work, and if everybody would also work, the nomination could be made. The work to be effected was not political log-rolling, but simply to convince the party represented there, and which had the honesty of a party representing a great principle and had never yet been in power, that Mr. Lincoln was the most available man. He seated himself behind a big table in the rooms of the headquarters and organized committees of visitation to the various delegations, and did the other work of the convention. For instance, he had Samuel C. Parks, of Logan, who was born in Vermont, organize a delegation of about four also from Vermont, to visit the delegates from that State; and he had me, from the State of Maine, organize a delegation, and visit my old friends from the Pine Tree State, and every man was to come back and report to him. And so he labored with all, issued his orders to all, and knew the situation of every delegation. He had Governor Oglesby, then of very stout lungs, fill the body of the building where the public were admitted, with a strong-voiced brigade of shouters. He organized at first two States—Illinois and Indiana—as presenting the name of Lincoln, and then had sporadic strength in almost every delegation. Pennsylvania had agreed, if on the second ballot we showed increasing strength, she would come to us with forty-eight votes.

I had the honor to be present with the judge and two leading delegates from Pennsylvania in the wee small hours of Friday morning, the day of the nomination, in which the question was whether Pennsylvania would not come on the second ballot and would not help to constitute the increase on that ballot. The result shows how well he succeeded. It is my belief if all the other causes had existed as they did exist, and Judge Davis had not lived, Mr. Lincoln would never have been nominated, and, consequently, never would have been elected President of the United States.

The leading candidates for the nomination for President, besides Lincoln, were William H. Seward, of New York; Salmon P. Chase, of Ohio; Simon Cameron, of Pennsylvania; Edward Bates, of Missouri; and John McLean, of Ohio. In a letter to an old friend, Hon. Josiah H. Drummond, of Portland, Maine, written from Bloomington on May 27th, Leonard Swett graphically described in further detail the tactics of the Illinois Delegation: [1]

[1] Oldroyd, O. H., *Lincoln's Campaign* (Chicago 1896) p. 71-73.

The first thing after getting our headquarters was to have the delegation proper invite the co-operation of outsiders as though they were delegates. Thus we began. The first State approached was Indiana. She was about equally divided between Bates and McLean. Saturday, Sunday and Monday were spent upon her, when finally she came to us unitedly with twenty-six votes, and from that time acted efficiently with us.

Seward came there with very nearly strength enough to nominate him, that is, men who intended to vote for him. Bates was the next strongest but that element was an opposition to Seward, because he was not available in the doubtful States, and would, as we well know, come to the winning man in opposition to him. Pennsylvania wanted Cameron, and insisted Seward would not carry that State. New Jersey wanted Dayton, and insisted Seward would not carry that State. So, the first point was gained, that is, the united assertion of the four doubtful States, Pennsylvania, New Jersey, Indiana and Illinois, that Seward would be defeated.

We let Greeley run his Bates machine, but got most of them for a second choice. Our programme was to give Lincoln 100 votes on the first ballot, with a certain increase afterwards, so that in the Convention our fortunes might seem to be rising, and thus catch the doubtful. Vermont had agreed to give us her second vote, so had Delaware, New Hampshire, an increase. It all worked to a charm. After the first days we were aided by the arrival of at least 10,000 people from Central Illinois and Indiana.

It was a part of the Seward plan to carry the Convention by outside pressure. Thursday the preliminary work was done. The friends of all parties Friday morning gathered to the capacious Wigwam. About 12,000 people were then inside and more out. A line of men were stationed on the roof, the nearest to the speaker's stand, catching from an open skylight the proceedings within and reporting to his next man, and so on to the man on the front of the building, who, with stentorian lungs, announced to the thousands in the street. Stores were closed, and, seemingly, the whole city was there.

First, opening the war, was the nomination of Seward. It was greeted with a deafening shout, which, I confess, appalled us a little. Afterward, Bates, McLean, Cameron and Chase came with moderate applause. Then came Lincoln, and our people tested their lungs. We beat them a little. They manifested this by seconding the nomination of Seward, which gave them another chance. It was an improvement upon the first, and placed us in the background. Caleb B. Smith, of Indiana, then seconded the nomination of Lincoln, and the West came to the rescue. No mortal eye before saw such a scene. The idea of our Hoosiers and Suckers being outscreamed would have been as bad to them as the loss of their man. Five thousand people at once leaped to their seats, women not wanting in the number, and the wild yell made soft whisper breathing of all that had preceded. No language can describe it. A thousand steam whistles, ten acres of hotel gongs, a tribe of Comanches, headed by a choice vanguard from pandemonium, might have mingled in the scene unnoticed.

This was not the most deliberate way of nominating a President, I will confess; but among other things, it had its weight, and I hope convinced the New York gentlemen that when they came West some other tactics must be resorted to.

Our increase after the first ballot was a little more than we calculated. On the third the ground swell was irresistible, and bore our man through, and the shout from the Wigwam and the shout from the street, as the man from the top shouted "Old Abe, hallelujah!" and the cannon with its mimic thunder, told the city and surroundings we had won.

The successful nomination and later election of Lincoln was beyond question chiefly the work of the three Bloomington men—David Davis, Leonard Swett and Jesse W. Fell. The first two were most in evidence at Chicago, while Mr. Fell conceived the plan and did most of the preliminary work. Mr. Fell devoted most of his time to field work, trying to secure full lists of names from the entire State for the literature sent out by the Republican National Committee. Always modest, Mr. Fell replied to the question of what part he took in the campaign of 1860, asked him by a distinguished Senator of the United States, as follows:[1]

Before responding to your inquiries, allow me to say, you give me much more credit than I am entitled to for the part I took in bringing before the American people the name of Abraham Lincoln as a candidate for the Presidency. Your original impressions were entirely correct. To Judge Davis more than any other man, living or dead, is the American people indebted for that extraordinary piece of good fortune, the nomination and consequent election of that man who combined in his person in so high a degree the elements necessary to a successful administration of the government through the late most critical period in our national history.

It is quite possible Mr. Lincoln's fitness, or rather availability, as a candidate for that position may have occurred to me before it did to the Judge, but at an early day—as early, I think, as 1858—it had his earnest approval, and I need not say his vastly superior influence gave to his opinion on this subject a weight and

[1] Duis, E., *Op. cit.,* p. 280.

character which my private and humble opinion could not command.

It is well known that Judge Davis, though not a delegate, was one of the leading men at the Decatur State Convention in May, 1860, that elected delegates to the Chicago National Convention; that he was there selected as one of the senatorial delegates to the latter body; that for more than a week prior to the nomination he had in connection with other friends of Mr. Lincoln, opened the "Lincoln Headquarters" at the Tremont House, Chicago, where, and throughout the city, wherever delegates were to be found, he labored day and night, almost sleeplessly, throughout that long and dramatically interesting contest, working with a zeal, assiduity and skill never surpassed, if ever equalled; and that when those herculean labors culminated in the choice of his trusted and most confidential friend, his feelings so overpowered him that not only then but for hours after, in grasping the hands of congratulating friends, he wept like a child.

Whilst it is undoubtedly true that, without the hearty and vigorous co-operation of quite a number of equally eminent men, the prestige attached to the names of Seward and others could not have been broken, and this nomination secured, no one, as familiar as I was with what was then and there enacted, can doubt for a moment the pre-eminent part there played by the Judge. Among Lincoln hosts he was emphatically the great central figure.

But in Mr. Fell's behalf we can quote Hon. James S. Ewing, also of Bloomington, who said: "I speak with some knowledge and with perfect sincerity when I say that, with the possible exception of the Hon. David Davis, Mr. Fell did more than any other man, living or dead, to secure the nomination of Mr. Lincoln to the presidency." [1]   In general, it was the lawyers and friends Lincoln had made while traveling the Eighth Judicial Circuit of Illinois, those men who knew him best, who gave him to the nation. (See Appendix III)

Reference has been made before to the importance of the continuity existing unbroken from the organization of the Republican Party at Bloomington in 1856 to the Republican Party of today. The crucial point in the history is the National Republican Convention of 1860. It is admitted that earlier local and State Republican meetings were held in Wisconsin and Michigan than in the State of Illinois, but it is denied that they have continuity with Republicanism today. The Republican Party of the present is the outgrowth of that party which nominated and elected Abraham Lincoln to the Presidency, just as present-day Christianity is an outgrowth of the Gentile Christianity of Paul rather than of the earlier Jewish Christianity which died out with the destruction of Jerusalem in the year 70 A. D. But Jewish Christianity had historical connection with Gentile Christianity, whereas Wisconsin and Michigan Republicanism did not have historical connection with Illinois Republicanism. The ballot records of the Chicago Convention show that both Wisconsin and Michigan voted

[1] Ewing, J. S. in Phillips, I. N., ed., *Op. cit.,* p. 57.

solidly for William H. Seward in all three ballots, which forfeits their claims for priority in founding the Republican Party. On the basis of continuity, therefore, the first Republican Convention which supported Abraham Lincoln must be considered the founder of the Republican Party of today, and on that basis the claim of the Bloomington Convention of 1856 cannot be disputed.

LI

ON June 2, 1860, a grand Republican rally for a Ratification meeting of Lincoln's nomination was held at Lincoln, Ill. Many prominent men spoke, including Leonard Swett of Bloomington. The whole State was invited to come with music and banners. Free trains were run from Bloomington to Lincoln and return, and the people of Bloomington turned out in great numbers to do honor to her hero.

LII

IN 1854 there was founded in New York City an organization of young men popularly called "Wide-Awakes," which was semi-military in character but strictly political in purpose. Originally belonging to the Whig Party, it be-

came strongly Republican.[1] Wide-Awake clubs
spread all over the country and took an active and
spectacular part in the 1860 campaign. On
Wednesday, June 6, 1860, the local Wide-Awake
club met at the Court House in Bloomington, at
which a Constitution was adopted containing the
following Preamble:[2]

We the undersigned citizens of Bloomington, desirous
of securing the ascendancy and perpetuity of the principles of the Republican Party, and the election of its
candidates for office to all places of honor and trust in
the Government, do hereby explicitly declare our devotion to the Constitution and the Union. Our opposition
to interference with Slavery in the States where it now
legally exists, and our unqualified and unalterable deter-
mination to resist by all constitutional means its further
extension . . .

The Railsplitter Wide-Awake Club of Springfield, Ill., planned a great Republican demonstration in Springfield on August 8, 1860, and sent
out letters of invitation to the various Wide-
Awake clubs of the State. The Bloomington Club
accepted with this letter:[3]

BLOOMINGTON, *August 7, 1860.*
L. ROSETTE, Secretary Wide-Awakes, Springfield, Ill.
Sir: We shall be down on the 11 A.M. train to-morrow
with some 125 torches, with Republican enthusiasm

[1] Scisco, L. D., *Political Nativism in New York State.* Columbia University, Studies in History, Economics and Public Law,
vol. xiii, no. 2 (New York 1901) p. 94-95.
[2] Bloomington *Daily Pantagraph,* June 9, 1860.
[3] Oldroyd, O. H., *Lincoln's Campaign,* p. 109.

enough for 1,000. Old McLean will send from 500 to 1,000 delegates.

Yours in the Republican cause for "Old Abe,"
S. B. BROWN,
Captain Bloomington Wide-Awake Club.

The Lincoln demonstration on the 8th was described by the *Illinois State Journal* (Springfield, Aug. 9th) as "a veritable political earthquake," and otherwise said: "We have no adequate words to describe what our eyes beheld." There were thousands upon thousands of people from all over the State, who formed a procession eight miles long that was headed by a large rolling ball, which symbolized the onward march of Republican principles. There were many speeches by prominent men, followed by a short acknowledgment by Abraham Lincoln. "But," according to the Bloomington *Pantagraph* of Aug. 10th, "the most brilliant and the most imposing sight of the kind ever witnessed in the country, was the torchlight procession of the Wide-Awakes at night. The procession was two miles long, when deployed, and the effect of their movements through the streets was most brilliant—illuminating the whole city." Thus did Bloomington and the State of Illinois again show loyalty to Abraham Lincoln!

LIII

AFTER a hard campaign,[1] the National election of 1860 was held on November 6th, at
which Lincoln was elected to the Presidency of
the United States. Of especial interest to us in
this connection is the comparison of the 1856 and
1860 votes for President in McLean County,
showing the growth of the Republican Party in
that County, as presented by the Bloomington
Daily Pantagraph of November 15, 1860:

The largest majorities attained by individual candidates on the Republican ticket in McLean county have
been as follows: In 1856 the largest majority was 580;
in 1858 it was 596; in 1859 it was 806; and in 1860 it
was 1000—a handsome increase.

In 1856, for President, Mr. Fremont received 1937
votes in this county; Mr. Buchanan, 1517, and Mr. Fillmore 566,—Mr. Fremont receiving 420 more than Mr.
Buchanan, and Mr. Buchanan and Mr. Fillmore together
receiving 146 more than Mr. Fremont.

In 1860, for President, Mr. Lincoln received 3553
votes in this county; Mr. Douglas, 2568; Mr. Bell, 58;
and Mr. Breckinridge, 7; Mr. Lincoln receiving 920
more than all the others together—the Republican candidate being stronger in this county in 1860 than in
1856 by 1066 votes. . . .

In 1856 the Presidential candidates received in this
county 4020 votes; in 1860 they received 6186; an increase of 2166 votes—more than one half in four years.

[1] Barringer, W. E., "Campaign Technique in Illinois—1860" in
Illinois State Historical Soc., *Transactions*, vol. xxxix (1932) p.
202-81.

While Lincoln received this large vote in Bloomington and McLean County, he won Springfield by only 69 votes and he lost his home county of Sangamon by 42 votes.[1] Bloomington and Springfield were poles apart in their respective feeling for and loyalty to Lincoln. From the very beginning to the fall elections of 1932, Bloomington and McLean County have been predominantly Republican!

LIV

ON the morning of November 21, 1860, Mr. and Mrs. Lincoln left Springfield for Chicago by train in order to meet the Vice-President-elect, Hannibal Hamlin. Efforts had been made to keep the trip from general knowledge, but crowds gathered at every station to welcome them as they passed through. At the town of Lincoln, the call for the President-elect was so persistent that he appeared and spoke a few words. At Bloomington a very large crowd gathered, and after many calls Lincoln spoke again, as follows:[2]

---

[1] Angle, P. M., *"Here I Have Lived"* (Springfield, Ill. 1935) p. 253n. Mr. Angle, in his "Prologue," greatly exaggerates the importance of Springfield in Lincoln's career, by crediting to that city various influences which were more a part of the Eighth Circuit as a whole or of Bloomington than they were of the town of Springfield itself.

[2] *New York Herald,* Nov. 22, 1860. Quoted in Lincoln, Abraham, *New Letters and Papers of Lincoln,* p. 258-59.

Fellow Citizens of Bloomington and McLean County:—I am glad to meet you after a longer separation than has been common between you and me. I thank you for the good report you made of the election in Old McLean. The people of the country have again fixed up their affairs for a constitutional period of time. By the way, I think very much of the people, as an old friend said he thought of woman. He said when he lost his first wife, who had been a great help to him in his business, he thought he was ruined—that he could never find another to fill her place. At length, however, he married another, who he found did quite as well as the first, and that his opinion now was that any woman would do well who was well done by. So I think of the whole people of this nation—they will ever do well if well done by. We will try to do well by them in all parts of the country, North and South, with entire confidence that all will be well with all of us.

While the train was at Bloomington a federal salute was fired, and then Senator Trumbull was called out for a brief response. Mrs. Lincoln, also, received quite an ovation in Bloomington, and she "bore herself admirably, bowing gracefully to the crowd, and shaking hands with those who approached her for that purpose in the car."

LV

AFTER the nomination of Lincoln, and even after his election, to the Presidency, his Bloomington friends Davis and Swett did not cease their labors in Lincoln's behalf. He needed advice on the state of the country and aid in the choice of his Cabinet. The greatest political "boss" in the United States was Thurlow Weed, Seward's campaign manager and the first Republican "boss" of the State of New York. After the nomination of Lincoln—but let Mr. Weed tell the story:[1]

Immediately after the nomination of Mr. Lincoln for President, at Chicago, in the summer of 1860, while annoyed and dejected at the defeat of Governor Seward, as I was preparing to shake the dust of the city from my feet, Messrs. David Davis (now a judge of the Supreme Court of the United States) and Leonard Swett called at my room. These gentlemen, warm friends and zealous supporters of Mr. Lincoln, had contributed more than all others to his nomination. After his name was presented as a candidate for President, and received with favor by the citizens of Illinois, Messrs. Davis and Swett visited Indiana, Ohio, Pennsylvania, and Maryland, for the purpose of commending Mr. Lincoln to the favorable consideration of prominent men in those states. They now called to converse with me about the approaching canvass. I informed them very frankly that I was so greatly disappointed at the result of the action of the convention as to be unable to think or talk on the subject; that I was going to pass a few days upon the prairies of Iowa, and that by the time I reached Albany I should be prepared to do my duty for the Republican cause and for its nominees. They then urged me to return home *via* Springfield, where we could talk over the canvass with Mr. Lincoln, saying that they would either join me at Bloomington, where they resided, or meet me at Springfield.

[1] Weed, Thurlow, *Autobiography of Thurlow Weed,* ed. by H. A. Weed (Boston 1883) p. 602-03.

After passing with a few friends a pleasant week in traveling through Iowa, I repaired to Springfield. There I found Messrs. Davis and Swett with Mr. Lincoln. . . . I found Mr. Lincoln sagacious and practical. He displayed throughout the conversation so much good sense, such intuitive knowledge of human nature, and such familiarity with the virtues and infirmities of politicians, that I became impressed very favorably with his fitness for the duties which he was not unlikely to be called upon to discharge. This conversation lasted some five hours, and when the train arrived in which we were to depart I rose all the better prepared to "go to work with a will" in favor of Mr. Lincoln's election, as the interview had inspired me with confidence in his capacity and integrity.

This conversation between Lincoln and Weed was so satisfactory that early in December, 1860, Lincoln desired to have another opportunity to benefit by the wisdom and experience of Weed. Leonard Swett tells us: [1]

About a month after the election the propriety of consulting Mr. Weed upon the formation of the Cabinet and the general condition of the country, which had begun to assume a threatening aspect, was under discussion. In conclusion, Mr. Lincoln asked me to write a letter to Mr. Weed, saying that he would like to see him, and asking him to come to Springfield for that purpose. I did so, [on Dec. 10, 1860] and in a few days he came to Bloomington, and Judge Davis and myself went to Springfield with him. Mr. Seward had already been selected, although, perhaps, no one knew it, and at the opening of the interview, Mr. Lincoln announced that fact. As to the rest of the Cabinet, it was an open ques-

[1] Barnes, T. W., *Memoir of Thurlow Weed* (Boston 1884) p. 293.

tion, although some names had been fixed upon, unless substantial objection should arise, and others were being favorably considered. Judge Davis and myself were present, by courtesy; but the substance of the interview was between Mr. Lincoln and Mr. Weed, and the object was to obtain his opinion upon all material questions connected with the opening of the administration. These interviews were protracted through several days, and every possible subject was discussed.

Thus did Lincoln's Bloomington friends secure for him the best political advice obtainable in the entire country, and changed a powerful political enemy into a valuable assistant!

LVI

ON February 11, 1861, Abraham Lincoln left Springfield for Washington, to take up his duties as President. With him, as a member of the official party, was Judge David Davis of Bloomington. The 4th of March following he became officially the President of the United States.

LVII

LINCOLN hardly had time to get established as President before the Civil War began by the firing upon Fort Sumter, on April 12, 1861. On the 15th President Lincoln issued a proclamation calling for 75,000 men, and on the following morning, in Bloomington, Jesse W. Fell called together a group of the leading men of the town, both Republicans and Democrats.[1] He had resolutions ready in support of the Union cause, which were favorably voted upon. A popular meeting was then called to take place in Phoenix Hall that night for the purpose of creating public sentiment in support of Lincoln, and speakers were chosen who could be relied upon. Next morning the *Pantagraph* stated:

On a notice of a few hours a monster meeting was held in this city last night, at Phœnix Hall, to give expression to the sentiments of our citizens on the National crisis now pending. It was a most harmonious, enthusiastic and glorious demonstration. Gentlemen of all parties, irrespective of former differences of political sentiments, met and participated in the proceedings as common patriots, loving their common country, and resolving alike to live in a common, *a whole* country, or to die if need be, for the preservation of that country.

Mr. Hamilton Spencer, Democrat, presided at the meeting, and Rev. Charles G. Ames presented the resolutions. The speakers included Rev. C. G. Ames and Ezra M. Prince, Republicans, and James S. Ewing and Dr. E. R. Roe, Democrats. The *Pantagraph* of the 18th supplemented its former notice of the meeting as follows:

[1] Morehouse, F. M. I., *Op. cit.*, p. 65-66.

Strangers to Bloomington may be interested in knowing that the Chairman of the meeting and of the resolution committee were leading Democrats (the latter a candidate on the State ticket at the last election), and that a majority of the Committee and of the speakers were prominent members of the same party here. It was indeed a complete fusion of parties in behalf of the Union.

This was the first public meeting in the State, following the fall of Fort Sumter, wherein the political parties laid aside their party affiliations and gave their unqualified support of the administration and the cause of the Union. Bloomington had not forgotten her Lincoln!

LVIII

ON February 4, 1861, the Eighth Judicial Circuit was reduced to the three counties of McLean, Logan and DeWitt (22 *Session Laws*, p. 100), and early in June David Davis was re-elected for the second time as Judge of the Circuit Courts. In the fall of that year Judge Davis was appointed Chairman of the "Western Commission" by President Lincoln to investigate claims against the Government for subsistence, clothing, transportation, arms, etc., which were needed for carrying on the War. The trouble was at St. Louis, and the investigation thus undertaken was thorough and exposed mismanagement and corruption of the Quartermaster's Department there.[1] Thus Lincoln early recognized the ability of Judge Davis, and was not disappointed.

LIX

B LOOMINGTON supported the War like a true and loyal friend of Lincoln. McLean County enrolled 6,866 soldiers, with an excess of credits (the largest number of any county in the State) of 160. Besides the lower ranks in the Army, Bloomington and the County supplied for the Union cause one Major-General, one Brevet Major-General, one Brigadier-General, two Brevet Brigadier-Generals and two Assistant Adjutant-Generals.[2] Judge Davis presided at the organization of Company E of the Ninety-fourth Infantry Regiment of Illinois, recruited at Phœnix Hall. So Bloomington did not fail when Lincoln's cause needed help!

LX

T HE loyal citizens of Bloomington held a meeting at Phœnix Hall on the evening of May 22, 1862, and organized by appointing U.

[1] Duis, E., *Op. cit.*, p. 281.
Dent, Thomas, *Op. cit.*, p. 543-44.
Pratt, H. E., *Op. cit.*, p. 169.
[2] McLean Co. Historical Society, *Op. cit.*, vol. i, p. 31.

F. Doubleday, president, Messrs. J. Bishop, K. H. Fell, E. M. Prince, J. Sparrow and S. P. Ives, vice-presidents, and J. A. Sewall, secretary. The following resolutions, among others, were then presented by the committee: [1]

Whereas, We regard the success of the government of the United States, in its present struggle to suppress the great Southern rebellion, as equally necessary to the national honor and safety, to the permanence of free government, and to the cause of christian civilization throughout the world; therefore,

Resolved, . . . 4th. That we regard the attempt to found a slave empire on the ruins of this republic, as a conspiracy against mankind, and as the greatest crime in history. . . .

6th. That the proposal for compensated emancipation, as suggested by the President and approved by Congress, meets our entire approval so far as it may apply to the slaves of loyal masters; and that we wish to see the doctrine that all slaves of rebels are legally and shall be forever free, fully carried out by the President, or by Act of Congress, in such form and under such conditions as shall be most likely to weaken the rebellion, and yet serve the permanent interests of both the white and black races.

Speeches were made by Messrs. E. M. Prince, C. G. Ames, F. J. Briggs, K. H. Fell, Willard, Herman Schroeder, of Bloomington, and a Mr. McGrew, of Galesburg. The resolutions were then unanimously adopted, and the meeting adjourned.

[1] Bloomington *Daily Pantagraph*, May 24, 1862.

LXI

IT was probably early in July, 1862, when an incident occurred which illustrates the struggle President Lincoln was having over the question of emancipation, and which confirms the confidence he had in his friend Leonard Swett. Mr. Swett in after years often told this story to his friends, and one of them, the Hon. Peter Stenger Grosscup, U. S. Circuit Judge for the Seventh Judicial Circuit, told it as given here: [1]

One day, during the course of the war, when Mr. Swett was at his home in Bloomington, Illinois, he received a telegram asking him to come immediately to the President. The second morning afterwards found him in Washington. Thinking that something unusual was at hand, he went to the White House upon arrival and before eating his breakfast. Mr. Lincoln asked him immediately into the cabinet room, and after making a few inquiries about mutual friends in Illinois, pulled up his chair to a little cabinet of drawers. Swett, of course, awaited in silence the developments. Opening a drawer, Lincoln took out a manuscript which, he said, was a letter from William Lloyd Garrison, and which he proceeded to read. It proved to be an eloquent and passionate appeal for the immediate emancipation of the slaves. It recalled the devotion and loyalty of the North, but pointed out, with something like peremptoriness, that unless some step was taken to cut out by the roots the institution of slavery, the expectations of the North would be disappointed and its ardor correspondingly

[1] Tarbell, I. M., *The Life of Abraham Lincoln,* vol. ii, p. 113-15.

cooled. It went into the moral wrong that lay at the bottom of the war, and insisted that the war could not, in the nature of things, be ended until the wrong was at an end. The letter throughout was entirely characteristic of Garrison.

Laying it back without comment, Mr. Lincoln took out another, which proved to be a letter from Garrett Davis, of Kentucky. It, too, treated of emancipation; but from the Border State point of view. It carefully balanced the martial and moral forces of the North and South, and pointed out that if the Border States, now divided almost equally between the belligerents, were thrown unitedly to the South, a conclusion of the war favorable to the North would be next to impossible. It then proceeded to recall that slavery was an institution of these Border States with which their people had grown familiar and upon which much of their prosperity was founded. Emancipation, especially emancipation without compensation, would, in that quarter of the country, be looked upon as a stab at prosperity and a departure from the original Union purposes of the war. It begged Mr. Lincoln to be led by the Northern abolition sentiment into no such irretrievable mistake.

Laying this back, Mr. Lincoln took out another, which turned out to be from a then prominent Swiss statesman, a sympathizer with the Northern cause, but whose name I cannot recall. It breathed all through an ardent wish that the North should succeed. The writer's purpose was to call attention to the foreign situation and the importance of preventing foreign intervention. This he summed up as follows: The governing classes in England and Napoleon in France were favorable to the success of the Confederacy. They were looking for a pretext upon which to base some sort of intervention. Anything that, in international law, would justify in-

tervention would be quickly utilized. A situation justi-
fying such a pretext must be avoided. The writer then
pointed out that from the earliest times any interference with the enemy's slaves had been regarded as a cruel
and improper expedient; that emancipation would be
represented to Europe as an equivalent of inciting slave
insurrection; and would be seized upon, the writer
feared, as a pretext upon which forcibly to intervene.
The letter went over the whole foreign situation, bringing out clearly this phase of the consequences of emancipation.

Laying this letter back, the President turned to Mr.
Swett, and without a word of inquiry, took up himself
the subject of emancipation, not only in the phases
pointed out by the letters just read, but every possible
phase and consequence under which it could be considered. For more than an hour he debated the situation,
first the one side and then the other of every question
arising. His manner did not indicate that he wished to
impress his views *upon* his hearer, but rather to weigh
and examine them for his own enlightenment *in the presence* of his hearer. It was an instance of stating conclusions aloud, not that they might convince another, or be
combatted by him, but that the speaker might see for
himself how they looked when taken out of the region of
mere reflection and embodied in words. The President's
deliverance was so judicial, and so free from the quality
of debate, or appearance of a wish to convince, that Mr.
Swett felt himself to be, not so much a hearer of Lincoln's
views, as a witness of the President's mental operations.
The President was simply framing his thought in
words, under the eye of his friend, that he might clear
up his own mind.

When the President concluded, he asked for no comment, and made no inquiry, but rising, expressed his

hope that Mr. Swett would get home safely, and entrusted to him some messages to their mutual friends. The audience thus ended.

A few days later, on July 22, 1862, President Lincoln called his Cabinet together and announced that he had decided to issue an Emancipation Proclamation, which he had already prepared, as soon as war conditions became favorable for such a step. Less than two months later the favorable time came with the victory at Antietam, and on September 22nd President Lincoln gave his second draft of the Emancipation Proclamation to the nation.

LXII

WHEN Lincoln became President he did not forget his friends in Illinois, especially the three Bloomington men who had done so much for him. It was unwise for him to include any of them in the Cabinet, as his own election to the Presidency had allowed Illinois all that was due her. But he wanted to reward them in some way. Jesse W. Fell was especially hard to provide for as he always modestly refused all preferment, but in March, 1862, Lincoln's opportunity came. Fell had arranged his nursery and real estate business for a long absence, and had offered his services for the war to President Lincoln. A letter from Lincoln to the Secretary of War, dated March 29, 1862, reads as follows: "I really wish Jesse W. Fell, of Illinois, to be appointed a Paymaster in the Regular Army, at farthest, as early as the 1st of July, 1862. I wish nothing to interfere with this; and I have so written as much as two months ago, I think." Mr. Fell accepted this appointment with the rank of Major, and served for eighteen months before he resigned.[1] This was all that Lincoln could do for Fell. Next David Davis was taken care of, but how is explained in a letter from Leonard Swett to Mr. Herndon:[2]

CHICAGO, ILL., *August 29, 1887.*

WILLIAM H. HERNDON.

My dear Sir:—Your inquiry in reference to the circumstances of the appointment of David Davis as one of the Justices of the Supreme Court reached me last evening. In reply I beg leave to recall the fact, that in 1860 the politicians of Illinois were divided into three divisions, which were represented in the Decatur convention by the votes on the nomination for Governor. The largest vote was for Norman B. Judd, of Chicago, his strength in the main being in the northern part of the State. I was next in order of strength, and Richard Yates the third, but the divisions were not materially unequal. The result was Yates was nominated, his strength being about Springfield and Jacksonville, extending to Quincy on the west, and mine was at Bloomington and vicinity and south and southeast.

These divisions were kept up awhile after Mr. Lincoln's election, and were considered in the distribution

[1] Morehouse, F. M. I., *Op. cit.,* p. 68.
[2] Herndon, W. H., *Op. cit.,* p. 405-08.

of Federal patronage. A vacancy in the United States Senate occurred early in 1861 by the death of Stephen A. Douglas, and Governor Yates appointed Oliver H. Browning, of Quincy, to fill the vacancy. There was also a vacancy upon the Supreme Bench of the United States to be filled from this general vicinity by Mr. Lincoln in the early part of his administration, and Judge Davis, of Bloomington, and Mr. Browning, of Quincy, were aspirants for the position. Mr. Browning had the advantage that Lincoln was new in his seat, and Senators were august personages; and, being in the Senate and a most courteous and able gentleman, Mr. Browning succeeded in securing nearly all the senatorial strength, and Mr. Lincoln was nearly swept off his feet by the current of influence. Davis' supporters were the circuit lawyers mainly in the eastern and central part of the State. These lawyers were at home, and their presence was not a living force felt constantly by the President at Washington.

I was then living at Bloomington, and met Judge Davis every day. As months elapsed we used to get word from Washington in reference to the condition of things; finally, one day the word came that Lincoln had said, "I do not know what I may do when the time comes, but there has never been a day when if I had to act I should not have appointed Browning." Judge Davis, General Orme, and myself held a consultation in my law-office at Bloomington. We decided that the remark was too Lincolnian to be mistaken and no man but he could have put the situation so quaintly. We decided also that the appointment was gone, and sat there glum over the situation. I finally broke the silence, saying in substance, "The appointment is gone and I am going to pack my carpet-sack for Washington." "No, you are not," said Davis. "Yes, I am," was my reply. "Lincoln is being swept off his feet by the influence of these Senators, and I will have the luxury of one more talk with him before he acts."

I did go home, and two days thereafter, in the morning about seven o'clock—for I knew Mr. Lincoln's habits well—was at the White House and spent most of the forenoon with him. I tried to impress upon him that he had been brought into prominence by the Circuit Court lawyers of the old eighth Circuit, headed by Judge Davis. "If," I said, "Judge Davis, with his tact and force, had not lived, and all other things had been as they were, I believe you would not now be sitting where you are." He replied gravely, "Yes, that is so." "Now it is a common law of mankind," said I, "that one raised into prominence is expected to recognize the force that lifts him, or, if from a pinch, the force that lets him out. The Czar Nicholas was once attacked by an assassin; a kindly hand warded off the blow and saved his life. The Czar hunted out the owner of that hand and strewed his pathway with flowers through life. The Emperor Napoleon III has hunted out everybody who even tossed him a biscuit in his prison at Ham and has made him rich. Here is Judge Davis, whom you know to be in every respect qualified for this position, and you ought in justice to yourself and public expectation to give him this place." We had an earnest pleasant forenoon, and I thought I had the best of the argument, and I think he thought so too.

I left him and went to Willard's Hotel to think over the interview, and there a new thought struck me. I therefore wrote a letter to Mr. Lincoln and returned to the White House. Getting in, I read it to him and left it with him. It was, in substance, that he might think if he gave Davis this place the latter when he got to Washington would not give him any peace until he gave me a place equally as good; that I recognized the fact that he could not give this place to Davis, which would be charged to the Bloomington faction in our State politics, and then give me anything I would have and be just to the party there; that this appointment, if made, should kill "two birds with one stone;" that I would accept it as one-half for me and one-half for the Judge; and that thereafter, if I or any of my friends ever troubled him, he could draw that letter as a plea in bar on that subject. As I read it Lincoln said, "If you mean that among friends as it reads I will take it and make the appointment." He at once did as he said.

He then made a request of the Judge after his appointment in reference to a clerk in his circuit, and wrote him a notice of the appointment, which Davis received the same afternoon I returned to Bloomington.

Judge Davis was about fifteen years my senior. I had come to his circuit at the age of twenty-four, and between him and Lincoln I had grown up leaning in hours of weakness on their own great arms for support. I was glad of the opportunity to put in the mite of my claims upon Lincoln and give it to Davis, and have been glad I did it every day since.

An unknown number of people have almost every week since, speaking perhaps extravagantly, asked me in a quasi-confidential manner, "How was it that you and Lincoln were so intimate and he never gave you anything?" I have generally said, "It seems to me that is my question, and so long as I don't complain I do not see why you should." I may be pardoned also for saying that I have not considered every man not holding an office out of place in life. I got my eyes open on this subject before I got an office, and as in Washington I saw the Congressman in decline I prayed that my latter end might not be like his.

Yours truly,
LEONARD SWETT.

It was in October, 1862, that Judge Davis was notified of his appointment to the Supreme Bench, and he resigned his office of Circuit Judge. He became associate Justice of the United States Supreme Court on December 8th. But Leonard Swett was not entirely ignored by President Lincoln. During the summer of 1863 Lincoln entrusted to Swett the settlement of the New Almaden Quicksilver Mining Co. litigation, of San Francisco, which netted Mr. Swett a very large fee.[1]

LXIII

THE Illinois state elections for congress in the fall of 1862 were important to our story. Two years earlier an eighth congressional district had been "made up" by Shelby M. Cullom, which contained the counties of Sangamon, Logan, DeWitt, McLean, Tazewell, Woodford and Livingston. Two of these counties were democratic, *i. e.,* Sangamon and Woodford. The fact that Sangamon was democratic illustrates again in how little regard Lincoln was held by his home county, in contrast to the loyalty he was always given in Bloomington! John T. Stuart of Springfield, Lincoln's former law partner, was chosen by the democratic convention on September 10th as its candidate in the Eighth District. Leonard

[1] Swett, L. H. in McLean Co. Historical Society, *Op. cit.,* vol. ii, p. 347.

Swett, of Bloomington, was the unanimous choice of the Union or Republican convention on September 24th. The campaign opened by the challenge of Mr. Swett to a series of joint debates, which Mr. Stuart refused.

The great issue between them was Lincoln's war policy and the Emancipation Proclamation. Stuart, because he was against the administration, was accused of pro-slavery views, but he indignantly denied the imputation. While he repeatedly declared his continued respect for Lincoln and "unbounding confidence . . . in his personal integrity," he could not approve of emancipation. He said that Lincoln violated the Constitution, which he did not believe was necessary. Swett, on the other hand, upheld Lincoln's conduct, and said "it is constitutional to use any means which may be found necessary."

Judge David Davis, shortly after he had been appointed to the Supreme Court, wrote a letter to the Bloomington *Pantagraph* on October 28th, in which he "desired the election of Mr. Swett." In the northern part of the district and outside of the towns the Republicans appeared to be strong, but Stuart relied on a large majority in Sangamon county to carry him to victory. Leonard Swett, throughout October and up to the eve of the election spoke in every hamlet and town in the district, and wound up as he had begun in Phoenix Hall in Bloomington.

On election day the state as a whole went largely democratic, and in the Eighth District Stuart polled 12,808 votes to 11,443 for Swett, a majority of 1,365 for Stuart. Thus did Lincoln's home county of Sangamon refuse to support his policies and friend. The result, however, might have been quite different had not 12,000 soldiers been absent from the district, of whom 8,000 were voters and at least 5,000 were in favor of the Union ticket.[1]

LXIV

ON December 5, 1862, Lieutenant-Colonel William McCullough of the Fourth Illinois Cavalry was killed in battle near Coffeville, Miss. He was a pioneer and one of the most popular men of Bloomington. In 1840 his right arm had been torn off by a threshing machine, but he was elected and served three successive terms as Sheriff of McLean County and then four successive terms as Clerk of the McLean County Circuit Court. In August, 1862, although he was fifty years of age, minus his right arm and with a defective eye, he enlisted in the army and served at Fort Henry and Fort Donelson, at Shiloh and at Corinth, with distinction and bravery. Upon news of his death, the bar of McLean County held a memorial meeting in his honor, at which

[1] Pratt, H E., "The Repudiation of Lincoln's War Policy in 1862 —Stuart-Swett Congressional Campaign" in Illinois State Historical Soc., *Journal,* vol. xxiv (1931-32) p. 129-40.

many legal lights spoke eloquently about him including Leonard Swett.[1]

Abraham Lincoln had known Mr. McCullough and his family for many years, and he was deeply affected by the tragedy. He wrote the following letter of condolence to the Colonel's daughter, who later became Mrs. Frank D. Orme of Washington:[2]

Executive Mansion, Washington,
Dec. 23, 1862.

Dear Fanny,—It is with deep regret that I learn of the death of your kind and brave father, and especially that it is affecting your young heart beyond what is common in such cases. In this sad world of ours sorrow comes to all, and to the young it comes with bitterer agony because it takes them unawares. The older have learned ever to expect it. I am anxious to afford some alleviation of your present distress. Perfect relief is not possible, except with time. You cannot now realize that you will ever feel better. Is not this so? And yet it is a mistake. You are sure to be happy again. To know this, which is certainly true, will make you some less miserable now. I have had experience enough to know what I say, and you need only to believe it to feel better at once. The memory of your dear father, instead of an agony, will yet be a sad, sweet feeling in your heart of a purer and holier sort than you have known before.

Please present my kind regards to your afflicted mother.

Your sincere friend,
A. Lincoln.

Miss Fanny McCullough,
   Bloomington, Ill.

[1] Duis, E., *Op. cit.,* p. 201-05.
[2] Lamon, W. H., *Recollections of Abraham Lincoln* (1911) p. 105-06.

Although Lamon calls this letter "peculiar,"
for some inexplicable reason, I think it is the most
tender and helpful letter of condolence I have
ever read. I consider it to be far superior to the
famous and perhaps spurious letter which Lincoln
is said to have written to Mrs. Lydia Bixby, nearly two years later, upon the supposed death of her
five sons on the field of battle. This in spite of the
fact that Henry Watterson called the latter "the
most sublime letter ever penned by the hand of
man."

LXV

THE year 1864 brought on another Presidential campaign, and as President Lincoln had
been severely criticised it seemed doubtful that he
would be renominated and reelected. In Bloomington, Phoenix Hall was Republican Headquarters again and the scene of many exciting meetings, while Jesse W. Fell stumped the State in
Lincoln's behalf. The campaign was successful,
with the result that Lincoln was renominated by
the Republican Party on the 7th of June and reelected by the nation on November 8th following.

LXVI

THE saddest day in United States history is
the 14th of April, 1865, when President Abraham Lincoln fell by an assassin's bullet. Nowhere

in the country was the blow felt more keenly than in Bloomington, Illinois, where Lincoln's dearest friends resided and where some of his greatest triumphs took place. Mr. John H. Burnham, a founder and officer of the McLean Co. Historical Society, has told the following story of how Bloomington learned of this sad event: [1]

When Mr. Lincoln was assassinated I was editor of the *Pantagraph*, then a mere miniature of the present important journal of that name. I had no assistant, was telegraph editor and proof reader, and was actually the whole editorial weakness. The morning after the assassination I was taking an early breakfast at the Briggs House, in Chicago. As I took my seat at the table, the sad, shocked appearance of the other persons present and their remarks led me to believe a murder had been committed in the hotel, but a remark overheard induced me to rush out for a morning paper. While hurriedly eating I read the remarkable news. Instantly I thought of the *Pantagraph*, and knowing in those times no dispatches ever reached the paper after midnight, its morning columns had contained no announcement of the tragedy. I began to study how I could furnish the quickest news to its readers. I knew that a dispatch containing such startling facts could be printed in a few minutes and be quickly circulated and thus give its readers near the center of town the important information long before the arrival of the Chicago papers. These papers then arrived in Bloomington about two o'clock in the afternoon. On my way to the C. & A. train, which was to leave Chicago a little after eight o'clock, I stopped at the Western Union Telegraph of-

[1] Burnham, J. H., in Bloomington High School *Aegis*, February 1906.

fice. The operator had not arrived, but the office was open and the porter was sweeping. I wrote a telegram of about 60 words, left my card with it on the operator's desk and just had time to catch my train. The operator must have entered a few minutes later, as my dispatch was sent promptly before the wires were busy. It was printed at the *Pantagraph* office so promptly that the "extra" was on the streets about nine o'clock. Crowds began to assemble around the square, and the people's grief and excitement knew no bounds. It seems that at the late breakfast table at the Ashley House, the predecessor of the Illinois Hotel, one of the boarders was heard to remark that Mr. Lincoln had gotten only what he deserved, or words to that effect. This was soon reported on the streets, probably with exaggerations, and a mob demanded his life. Public feeling ran so high that it seemed as if a victim was instantly needed to pacify the wrath of Bloomington, and there were but few heads cool enough to stem the storm. Men like Kersey H. Fell, Judge John E. McClun and a few others were cool and contrived to have the mob agree to a form of trial to investigate and report the exact language used. A committee composed of men in whom all parties had confidence was chosen, and while they were attending to the trial, the man's friends who were very much afraid that a correct report of his language would be his death warrant, smuggled him down the back stairs of the hotel and into a covered carriage and had him conveyed so far towards Peoria by the time the committee was ready to report that the mob became quieter and cooler, and no further attempt was made to find the victim. Bloomington breathed much freer to find that its agony of grief had not been stained by frenzied bloodshed.

When the Chicago train arrived at about two o'clock in the afternoon, I brought my copy of the *Tribune* up town, and while the 100 or more Chicago papers were being folded and prepared for distribution by Dalton and Dibble at their news store on the west side of the square, Thomas W. Tipton, one of our young lawyers, afterwards Judge Tipton, who died only a few years ago, was compelled by the crowd to stand on top of the wooden post at the southwest corner of the courthouse square and read my *Tribune* to the sad and impatient multitude.

Much more might be added, but enough has been said to show how the great heart of Bloomington throbbed with sorrow in April, 1865.

On Sunday, April 16th, an Indignation Meeting was held in the Court House Square to express the sorrow of the town. Many of Lincoln's friends spoke, and the immediate death of the assassin, John Wilkes Booth, was called for.

Then began the mournful and slow passage of the train which bore Lincoln's body from Washington to his home-city, Springfield, Illinois, for burial. The funeral train, with Judge David Davis aboard, was scheduled to pass through Bloomington at 4.43 o'clock in the morning on Wednesday, May 3, 1865. Bells of the city were rung about 3 A. M. to awaken the citizens, and three or four thousand people assembled at the station of the Chicago, Alton & St. Louis Railroad. The train did not arrive according to schedule, however, and it was after sunrise before it passed through the city. Although there was no systematic display, a spontaneous outpouring of sympathy was taken for granted by the presence

From photograph by John S. Scibird

INDIGNATION MEETING IN COURT HOUSE SQUARE, BLOOMINGTON, ILLINOIS, AFTER ASSASSINATION OF LINCOLN
(Easter Sunday, April 16, 1865)

1—Court House. 2—Court House Annex. 3—Office in Court House Yard. 4—M. E. Church. 5—First National Bank. 6—Hyde's Tailor Shop, Ward's Tailor Shop on second floor. 7—Phoenix Block.

of so many people at such an early hour.[1] Lincoln's funeral was held at Springfield on May 4th, and at least 1,000 Bloomingtonians went to Springfield to attend. It was like Sunday in Bloomington on that day, as all business was suspended and the schools were closed. No newspapers were issued in the city the following day, so as to permit the paper employees to attend the funeral. Later, when a national subscription was taken up to place a monument over Lincoln's grave, Bloomington arranged benefits for and subscribed to the fund. Thus even after his death was Bloomington loyal to Lincoln!

LXVII

PRESIDENT Lincoln left no will; but after his death, at the request of Mrs. Lincoln and their son, Robert, David Davis of Bloomington was appointed administrator of Mr. Lincoln's Estate.[2] In an address before the bar at Indianapolis, on May 19, 1865, David Davis paid the following tribute to Lincoln:[3]

[1] Bloomington *Daily Pantagraph,* May 4, 1865. Mr. Rexford Newcomb (*In the Lincoln Country,* p. 149) says that Lincoln's body lay in state in Bloomington on the way to Springfield for burial. I find no evidence for this view, and the Bloomington paper gives the version I have presented.

[2] The Inventory of Lincoln's estate, as made by David Davis, may be found in Sandburg, Carl, and Angle, P. M., *Mary Lincoln: Wife and Widow* (New York 1932) p. 270-74.

[3] Nicolay, J. G. and Hay, John, *Abraham Lincoln: a History.* 10 vols. (New York 1890) vol. i, p. 301-03.

I enjoyed for over a quarter of a century the personal friendship of Mr. Lincoln. We were admitted to the bar about the same time and traveled for many years what is known in Illinois as the Eighth Judicial Court. In 1848, when I first went on the bench, the circuit embraced fourteen counties, and Mr. Lincoln went with the Court to every county. Railroads were not then in use, and our mode of travel was either on horseback or in buggies.

This simple life he loved, preferring it to the practice of the law in a city, where, although the remuneration would be greater, the opportunity would be less for mixing with the great body of the people, who loved him, and whom he loved. Mr. Lincoln was transferred from the bar of that circuit to the office of the President of the United States, having been without official position since he left Congress in 1849. In all the elements that constitute the great lawyer he had few equals. He was great both at *nisi prius* and before an appellate tribunal. He seized the strong points of a cause, and presented them with clearness and great compactness. His mind was logical and direct, and he did not indulge in extraneous discussion. Generalities and platitudes had no charms for him. An unfailing vein of humor never deserted him; and he was able to claim the attention of court and jury, when the cause was the most uninteresting, by the appropriateness of his anecdotes.

His power of comparison was large, and he rarely failed in a legal discussion to use that mode of reasoning. The framework of his mental and moral being was honesty, and a wrong cause was poorly defended by him. The ability which some eminent lawyers possess, of explaining away the bad points of a cause by ingenious sophistry, was denied him. In order to bring into full activity his great powers, it was necessary that he should be convinced of the right and justice of the matter which he advocated. When so convinced, whether the cause was great or small, he was usually successful. He read law-books but little, except when the cause in hand made it necessary; yet he was usually self-reliant, depending on his own resources, and rarely consulting his brother lawyers, either on the management of his case or on the legal questions involved.

Mr. Lincoln was the fairest and most accommodating of practitioners, granting all favors which were consistent with his duty to his client, and rarely availing himself of an unwary oversight of his adversary.

He hated wrong and oppression everywhere, and many a man whose fraudulent conduct was undergoing review in a court of justice has writhed under his terrific indignation and rebukes. He was the most simple and unostentatious of men in his habits, having few wants, and those easily supplied. To his honor be it said that he never took from a client, even when his cause was gained, more than he thought the services were worth and the client could reasonably afford to pay. The people where he practiced law were not rich, and his charges were always small. When he was elected President, I question whether there was a lawyer in the circuit, who had been at the bar so long a time, whose means were not larger. It did not seem to be one of the purposes of his life to accumulate a fortune. In fact, outside of his profession, he had no knowledge of the way to make money, and he never even attempted it.

Mr. Lincoln was loved by his brethren of the bar, and no body of men will grieve more at his death, or pay more sincere tributes to his memory. His presence on the circuit was watched for with interest and never failed to produce joy or hilarity. When casually absent, the spirits of both bar and people were depressed. He was not fond of litigation, and would compromise a lawsuit whenever practicable.

And I may be permitted to say here that the great qualities of his mind and heart preeminently fitted him to settle the questions growing out of this war, to readjust the displaced machinery of government, and to reunite a divided people. War with him was simply a necessity for the sake of peace. It has seemed to me that the atrocity of the crime which deprived him of life was only excelled by its folly. He loved his profession, appreciating the high services always rendered by it to the cause of good government and civil liberty. To elucidate truth was a precious privilege with him, and he was always glad to avail himself of it. He was kind and gentle in his nature, with sympathies easily awakened, "with charity for all, and malice to none," harboring no resentment to opposing counsel, and indulgent to his younger brethren.

Mr. Lincoln's whole life attests the strength and sincerity of his convictions. Although ambitious, yet office had no attractions for him, if attainable through a sacrifice of principle. He attached himself to a party, when satisfied that its views of public policy were correct, and the circumstance that the party was in the minority, and could with difficulty win its way to the confidence of the people, had no terrors for him. Had he loved principle less and place more, he would not have been without official station during the greater portion of his life.

He had faith—without which true greatness does not exist. Believing in certain great principles of government, he did not complain because for a season, they were unacceptable to the people—having faith in their ultimate triumph.

Mr. Lincoln was daily growing in wisdom, and greatness, and was fast gaining the confidence and attachment of the whole American people. He died at the most critical period in the history of the nation, when it was apparent that his country would be free from the curse

and disgrace of slavery. Had he survived to complete
the work he had begun, it is easy to see that the basis,
which in his wisdom he should have thought proper to
adopt to settle our difficulties, would have been accepted
by the country, and that all factious opposition to his
administration would have ceased. Hereafter the name
of Abraham Lincoln will be associated with that of
George Washington, and the present and all future
generations will equally honor and revere them.[1]

LXVIII

IN the latter part of the year 1865 Leonard
Swett moved to Chicago from Bloomington,
made necessary by his increasing reputation as a
lawyer. In a letter to Herndon, dated January
17, 1866, Mr. Swett gave the following estimate
of and tribute to Abraham Lincoln:[2]

Lincoln's whole life was a calculation of the law of
forces and ultimate results. The whole world to him
was a question of cause and effect. He believed the results to which certain causes tended; he did not believe
that those results could be materially hastened or im-
peded. His whole political history, especially since the
agitation of the slavery question, has been based upon
this theory. He believed from the first, I think, that the
agitation of slavery would produce its overthrow, and
he acted upon the result as though it was present from

[1] The last four paragraphs are taken from the transcript of the
address in the Indianapolis *Daily Sentinel* for May 20, 1865. They
are not included in the Nicolay and Hay work, and so far as the
author is aware have not been previously published.

[2] Herndon, W. H., *Op. cit.,* p. 425-32.

the beginning. His tactics were to get himself in the right place and remain there still, until events would find him in that place. This course of action led him to say and do things which could not be understood when considered in reference to the immediate surroundings in which they were done or said. You will remember, in his campaign against Douglas in 1858, the first ten lines of the first speech he made defeated him. The sentiment of the "house divided against itself" seemed wholly inappropriate. It was a speech made at the commencement of a campaign, and apparently made for the campaign. Viewing it in this light alone, nothing could have been more unfortunate or inappropriate. It was saying just the wrong thing; yet he saw it was an abstract truth, and standing by the speech would ultimately find him in the right place. I was inclined at the time to believe these words were hastily and inconsiderately uttered, but subsequent facts have convinced me they were deliberate and had been matured. Judge T. L. Dickey says, that at Bloomington, at the first Republican Convention in 1856, he uttered the same sentences in a speech delivered there, and that after the meeting was over, he (Dickey) called his attention to these remarks. Lincoln justified himself in making them by stating they were true; but finally, at Dickey's urgent request, he promised that for his sake, or upon his advice, he would not repeat them. . . .

He never believed in political combinations, and consequently, whether an individual man or class of men supported or opposed him, never made any difference in his feelings, or his opinions of his own success. If he was elected, he seemed to believe that no person or class of persons could ever have defeated him, and if defeated, he believed nothing could ever have elected him. Hence, when he was a candidate, he never wanted anything done for him in the line of political combination or management. He seemed to want to let the whole subject alone, and for everybody else to do the same. I remember, after the Chicago Convention, when a great portion of the East were known to be dissatisfied at his nomination, when fierce conflicts were going on in New York and Pennsylvania, and when great exertions seemed requisite to harmonize and mould in concert the action of our friends, Lincoln always seemed to oppose all efforts made in the direction of uniting the party. I arranged with Mr. Thurlow Weed after the Chicago Convention to meet him at Springfield. I was present at the interview, but Lincoln said nothing. It was proposed that Judge Davis should go to New York and Pennsylvania to survey the field and see what was necessary to be done. Lincoln consented, but it was always my opinion that he consented reluctantly.

He saw that the pressure of a campaign was the external force coercing the party into unity. If it failed to produce that result, he believed any individual effort would also fail. If the desired result followed, he considered it attributable to the great cause, and not aided by the lesser ones. He sat down in his chair in Springfield and made himself the Mecca to which all politicians made pilgrimages. He told them all a story, said nothing, and sent them away. All his efforts to procure a second nomination were in the same direction. I believe he earnestly desired that nomination. He was much more eager for it than he was for the first, and yet from the beginning he discouraged all efforts on the part of his friends to obtain it. From the middle of his first term all his adversaries were busily at work for themselves. Chase had three or four secret societies and an immense patronage extending all over the country. Fremont was constantly at work, yet Lincoln would never do anything either to hinder them or to help himself.

He was considered too conservative, and his adversaries were trying to outstrip him in satisfying the radical element. I had a conversation with him upon this subject in October, 1863, and tried to induce him to recommend in his annual message a constitutional amendment abolishing slavery. I told him I was not very radical, but I believed the result of the war would be the extermination of slavery; that Congress would pass the amendment making the slave free, and that it was proper at that time to be done. I told him also, if he took that stand, it was an outside position, and no one could maintain himself upon any measure more radical, and if he failed to take the position, his rivals would. Turning to me suddenly he said, "Is not the question of emancipation doing well enough now?" I replied it was. "Well," said he, "I have never done an official act with a view to promote my own personal aggrandizement, and I don't like to begin now. I can see that emancipation is coming; whoever can wait for it will see it; whoever stands in its way will be run over by it."

His rivals were using money profusely; journals and influences were being subsidized against him. I accidentally learned that a Washington newspaper, through a purchase of the establishment, was to be turned against him, and consulted him about taking steps to prevent it. The only thing I could get him to say was that he would regret to see the paper turned against him. Whatever was done had to be done without his knowledge. Mr. Bennett of the *Herald*, with his paper, you know, is a power. The old gentleman wanted to be noticed by Lincoln, and he wanted to support him. A friend of his, who was certainly in his secrets, came to Washington and intimated if Lincoln would invite Bennett to come over and chat with him, his paper would be all right. Mr. Bennett wanted nothing, he simply wanted to be noticed. Lincoln in talking about it said, "I understand it; Bennett has made a great deal of money, some say not very properly, now he wants me to make him respectable. I have never invited Mr. Bryant or Mr. Greeley here; I shall not, therefore, especially invite Mr. Bennett." All Lincoln would say was, that he was receiving everybody, and he should receive Mr. Bennett if he came.

Notwithstanding his entire inaction, he never for a moment doubted his second nomination. One time in his room discussing with him who his real friends were, he told me, if I would not show it, he would make a list of how the Senate stood. When he got through, I pointed out some five or six, and I told him I knew he was mistaken about them. Said he, "You may think so, but you keep that until the convention and tell me then whether I was right." He was right to a man. He kept a kind of account book of how things were progressing, for three or four months, and whenever I would get nervous and think things were going wrong, he would get out his estimates and show how everything on the great scale of action, such as the resolutions of legislatures, the instructions of delegates, and things of that character, were going exactly as he expected. These facts, with many others of a kindred nature, have convinced me that he managed his politics upon a plan entirely different from any other man the country has ever produced.

He managed his campaigns by ignoring men and by ignoring all small causes, but by closely calculating the tendencies of events and the great forces which were producing logical results.

In his conduct of the war he acted upon the theory that but one thing was necessary, and that was a united North. He had all shades of sentiments and opinions to deal with, and the consideration was always presented to his mind, how can I hold these discordant elements together?

It was here that he located his own greatness as a President. One time, about the middle of the war, I left his house about eleven o'clock at night, at the Soldiers' Home. We had been discussing the discords in the country, and particularly the States of Missouri and Kentucky. As we separated at the door he said, "I may not have made as great a President as some other men, but I believe I have kept these discordant elements together as well as anyone could." Hence, in dealing with men he was a trimmer, and such a trimmer the world has never seen. Halifax, who was great in his day as a trimmer, would blush by the side of Lincoln; yet Lincoln never trimmed in principles, it was only in his conduct with men. He used the patronage of his office to feed the hunger of these various factions. Weed always declared that he kept a regular account-book of his appointments in New York, dividing his various favors so as to give each faction more than it could get from any other source, yet never enough to satisfy its appetite.

They all had access to him, they all received favors from him, and they all complained of ill treatment; but while unsatisfied, they all had "large expectations," and saw in him the chance of obtaining more than from anyone else whom they could be sure of getting in his place. He used every force to the best possible advantage. He never wasted anything, and would always give more to his enemies than he would to his friends; and the reason was, because he never had anything to spare, and in the close calculation of attaching the factions to him, he counted upon the abstract affection of his friends as an element to be offset against some gift with which he must appease his enemies. Hence, there was always some truth in the charge of his friends that he failed to reciprocate their devotion with his favors. The reason was, that he had only just so much to give away—"He always had more horses than oats."

An adhesion of all forces was indispensable to his success and the success of the country; hence he husbanded his means with the greatest nicety of calculation. Adhesion was what he wanted; if he got it gratuitously he never wasted his substance paying for it.

His love of the ludicrous was not the least peculiar of his characteristics. His love of fun made him overlook everything else but the point of the joke sought after. If he told a good story that was refined and had a sharp point, he did not like it any the better because it was refined. If it was outrageously vulgar, he never seemed to see that part of it, if it had the sharp ring of wit; nothing ever reached him but the wit. Almost any man that will tell a very vulgar story, has, in a degree, a vulgar mind; but it was not so with him; with all his purity of character and exalted morality and sensibility, which no man can doubt, when hunting for wit he had no ability to discriminate between the vulgar and the refined substances from which he extracted it. It was the wit he was after, the pure jewel, and he would pick it up out of the mud or dirt just as readily as he would from a parlor table.

He had great kindness of heart. His mind was full of tender sensibilities, and he was extremely humane, yet while these attributes were fully developed in his character, and, unless intercepted by his judgment, controlled him, they never did control him contrary to his judgment. He would strain a point to be kind, but he never strained it to breaking. Most men of much kindly feeling are controlled by this sentiment against their judgment, or rather that sentiment beclouds their judgment. It was never so with him; he would be just as kind and generous as his judgment would let him be—no more. If he ever deviated from this rule, it was to save life. He would sometimes, I think, do things he knew to be impolitic and wrong to save some poor fellow's neck. I remember one day being in his room when he was sitting at his table with a large pile of papers before him, and after a pleasant talk he turned quite abruptly and said, "Get out of the way, Swett; to-morrow is butcher-day, and I must go through these papers and see if I cannot find some excuse to let these poor fellows off." The pile of papers he had were the records of courts martial of men who on the following day were to be shot. He was not examining the records to see whether the evidence sustained the findings; he was purposely in search of occasions to evade the law, in favor of life.

Some of Lincoln's friends have insisted that he lacked the strong attributes of personal affection which he ought to have exhibited; but I think this is a mistake. Lincoln had too much justice to run a great government for a few favors; and the complaints against him in this regard, when properly digested, seem to amount to this and to no more, that he would not abuse the privileges of his situation.

He was certainly a very poor hater. He never judged men by his like or dislike for them. If any given act was to be performed, he could understand that his enemy could do it just as well as anyone. If a man had maligned him or been guilty of personal ill-treatment, and was the fittest man for the place, he would give him that place just as soon as he would give it to a friend.

I do not think he ever removed a man because he was his enemy or because he disliked him.

The great secret of his power as an orator, in my judgment, lay in the clearness and perspicuity of his statements. When Mr. Lincoln had stated a case it was always more than half argued and the point more than half won. It is said that some one of the crowned heads of Europe proposed to marry when he had a wife living. A gentleman, hearing of this proposition, replied, how could he? "Oh," replied his friend, "he could marry and then he could get Mr. Gladstone to make an explanation about it." This was said to illustrate the convincing power of Mr. Gladstone's statement.

Mr. Lincoln had this power greater than any man I have ever known. The first impression he generally conveyed was, that he had stated the case of his adversary better and more forcibly than his opponent could state it himself. He then answered that statement of facts fairly and fully, never passing by or skipping over a bad point.

When this was done he presented his own case. There was a feeling, when he argued a case, in the mind of any man who listened to it, that nothing had been passed over; yet if he could not answer the objections he argued, in his own mind, and himself arrive at that conclusion to which he was leading others, he had very little power of argumentation. The force of his logic was in conveying to the minds of others the same clear and thorough analysis he had in his own, and if his own mind failed to be satisfied, he had little power to satisfy anybody else. He never made a sophistical argument in his life, and never could make one. I think he was of less real aid in trying a thoroughly bad case than any man I was ever associated with. If he could not grasp the whole case and believe in it, he was never inclined to touch it.

From the commencement of his life to its close, I have sometimes doubted whether he ever asked anybody's advice about anything. He would listen to everybody; he would hear everybody; but he rarely, if ever, asked for opinions. I never knew him in trying a case to ask the advice of any lawyer he was associated with.

As a politician and as President, he arrived at all his conclusions from his own reflections, and when his opinion was once formed, he never doubted but what it was right.

One great public mistake of his character, as generally received and acquiesced in, is that he is considered by the

people of this country as a frank, guileless and unso-
phisticated man. There never was a greater mistake. Beneath a smooth surface of candor and apparent declaration of all his thoughts and feelings, he exercised the most
exalted tact and the wisest discrimination. He handled
and moved men remotely as we do pieces upon a chess-
board. He retained through life all the friends he ever
had, and he made the wrath of his enemies to praise him.
This was not by cunning or intrigue, in the low accepta-
tion of the term, but by farseeing reason and discern-
ment. He always told enough only of his plans and purposes to induce the belief that he had communicated all,
yet he reserved enough to have communicated nothing.
He told all that was unimportant with a gushing frank-
ness, yet no man ever kept his real purposes closer, or
penetrated the future further with his deep designs.

Thus did two of the men who knew Lincoln best
and loved him most pay tribute to his memory.

LXIX

ALL but the conclusion has now been told.
David Davis was still serving as an Associate
Justice of the Supreme Court of the United
States when, on February 21, 1872, he was nom-
inated for President of the United States by the
National Convention of the Labor Reform Party,
at Columbus, Ohio, but he declined the honor. In
May of the same year his name was also presented
for nomination for the same office by the National
Convention of Liberal Republicans, at Cincin-
nati, Ohio, but without success. However, on

January 25, 1877, Judge Davis was elected U. S. Senator from Illinois for a period of six years, and on March 4th he resigned as Justice to accept his new position. When a special session of the Senate convened October 10, 1881, the office of Vice-President of the United States was temporarily vacant, due to the death of President James A. Garfield and to Vice-President Arthur succeeding to his place. Accordingly Senator Davis was elected President of the Senate (Vice-President of the United States) *pro temp,* and for the remainder of his term as Senator he occupied that position. His term as Senator expired in March, 1883, and in 1884 he was elected President of the Illinois State Bar Association. David Davis died at his home in Bloomington on June 26, 1886, after an illness of several months.

LXX

AFTER the Civil War, Jesse W. Fell continued his many public services in helping to fight the political battles of his friends and improving the city of Bloomington. He acted upon his version of an old couplet:

> He who plants a tree (*and cares for it*)
> Does something for posterity.

Bloomington owes more to Jesse W. Fell than to any other man. He died on February 25, 1887, mourned by all who knew him. On June 5, 1916, a Jesse W. Fell Memorial Gateway was dedicated on the campus of the Illinois State Normal University at Normal, a suburb of Bloomington.[1] The tablet reads as follows:

TO THE FOUNDER OF NORMAL
JESSE W. FELL,
FRIEND OF EDUCATION,
LOVER AND PLANTER OF TREES,
PHILANTHROPIST OF MIGHTY VISION,
THIS GATE IS DEDICATED BY
THE WOMAN'S IMPROVEMENT LEAGUE
AND HIS MANY FRIENDS.

LXXI

IN Chicago, Leonard Swett had a long and brilliant legal career. Outside of his practice he was in great demand as a speaker, and when, in October, 1887, St. Gaudens' great statue of Abraham Lincoln was unveiled in Lincoln Park, Chicago, Mr. Swett delivered the oration of the day, at the joint request of the monument association and the Lincoln Park commission. The Chicago *Times and Tribune,* of October 23, 1887, stated:

Never since the night of the great fire of 1871, had Lincoln Park ever contained within the same area so

[1] "Jesse W. Fell Memorial Gateway, State Normal University Campus" in Illinois State Historical Soc., *Journal,* vol. ix (1916-17) p. 321-43.

many human beings as thronged its plains, clustered under its trees, and in every variety of vehicle crowded its roadways. Amid the roar of cannon, the triumphal strains of national airs, the cheers of thousands, and the tears of many, the colossal bronze figure was unveiled, and the oration of Leonard Swett, Lincoln's old friend, was worthy of the theme and the occasion.

During the latter years of his life Mr. Swett's health was undermined by overwork, and while he was preparing to visit Europe for a rest he was stricken and died June 8, 1889. With him passed the last of the great Lincoln Triumvirate.

LXXII

BLOOMINGTON, Illinois, has been very proud of her contributions of eminent people to the life of the nation, which is all out of proportion in glory to the size of the city which gave them. She numbers among her citizens Vice-Presidents of the United States, United States Senators, Governors of States, Congressmen, State Senators, playwrights, actors and actresses, Generals and other high military officials, authors, musicians, railroad Presidents, Judges and lawyers, etc., all of national and some even of international fame. Yet in all the list, Bloomington has regretted that a President of the United States is not to be numbered. This city, however, need be sorrowful no longer; she can hold her head high in any company! The greatest President the United States ever had is her own peculiar gift to the nation, and she can ever be proud of the glorious name of Abraham Lincoln!

APPENDIX

I

LINCOLN'S "PEORIA SPEECH" IN BLOOMINGTON

Since it is a discovery of the author that Lincoln delivered what is known as his famous "Peoria Speech" in Bloomington on September 12, 1854, over a month before its presentation in Peoria, it seems well to furnish the evidence for this assertion. Accordingly I present in parallel columns the newspaper report of Lincoln's speech in Bloomington,[1] and the passages in the "Peoria Speech" which conform to that address as described:[2]

Bloomington Speech	*"Peoria Speech"*
He first declared that the Southern slaveholders were neither better, nor worse than we of the North, and that we of the North were no better than they. If we were situated as they are, we should act and feel as they do; and if they were situated as we are, they should act and feel as we do; and we never ought to lose sight of this fact in discussing the subject. With slavery as existing in the slave States at the time of	Before proceeding let me say that I think I have no prejudice against the Southern people. They are just what we would be in their situation. If slavery did not now exist among them, they would not introduce it. If it did now exist among us, we should not instantly give it up. This I believe of the masses North and South. . . . They [the fathers of the republic] found the institution [slavery] existing among us, which they could

[1] Bloomington *Weekly Pantagraph,* Sept. 20, 1854, as quoted in Lincoln, Abraham, *New Letters and Papers of Lincoln,* p. 133-37.
[2] Lincoln, Abraham, *Complete Works,* vol. ii, p. 190-248.

the formation of the Union, he had nothing to do. There was a vast difference between tolerating it there, and protecting the slave-holder in the rights granted him by the Constitution, and extending slavery over a territory already free, and uncontaminated with the institution. When our federal compact was made, almost all of the valley of the Mississippi belonged to the French, not us; and what little territory we had belonged to different States; Virginia owning almost all of what now constitutes the States of Ohio, Indiana, Illinois, Michigan, and Wisconsin. Thomas Jefferson, being a Virginian, proposed the cession of this territory to the general government, and in carrying out the measure, had the clause especially inserted, that slavery should never be introduced into it. Kentucky belonged also to Virginia, but was settled as a part of the State of Virginia, so that slavery was carried there by the first settlers from Virginia, and was admitted into the Union with the institution as existing there. Tennessee be-

not help. . . .

But all this, to my judgment, furnishes no more excuse for permitting slavery to go into our own free territory than it would for reviving the African slave-trade by law.

When we established our independence, we did not own or claim the country to which this compromise applies. Indeed, strictly speaking, the confederacy then owned no country at all; the States respectively owned the country within their limits, and some of them owned territory beyond their strict State limits. Virginia thus owned the Northwestern territory—the country out of which the principal part of Ohio, all Indiana, all Illinois, all Michigan, and all Wisconsin have since been formed. . . . The question of ceding the territories to the General Government was set on foot. Mr. Jefferson,—a Virginian by birth,—conceived the idea of taking that occasion to prevent slavery ever going into the Northwestern Territory. . . . She also owned (perhaps within her then limits) what has since been formed into the State of longed to North Carolina, and was settled by emigrants from that State, and was admitted into the Union as Kentucky was. Alabama was settled from South Carolina and admitted in a similar manner. Thus three slave States were made from territories that belonged to i n d i v i d u a l slaveholding States.

Jefferson saw the necessity of our government possessing the whole valley of the Mississippi; and though he acknowledged that our Constitution made no provision for the purchasing of territory, yet he thought that the exigency of the case would justify the measure, and the purchase was made. When the lower part of this territory comprising the State of Louisiana, wished to be admitted, the institution of slavery having existed there long before the territory was bought, she was admitted with the institution without any opposition, as a right that belonged to her citizens.

There was an old French settlement in St. Louis and vicinity, with slaves; and that territory comprising

Kentucky. North Carolina thus owned what is now the State of Tennessee; and South Carolina and Georgia owned, in separate parts, what are now Mississippi and Alabama. . . .

He [Jefferson] prevailed on the Virginia legislature to adopt his views, and to cede the Territory. . . . Congress accepted the cession . . .; and the first ordinance (which the acts of Congress were then called) for the government of the Territory p r o v i d e d that slavery should never be permitted therein. This is the famed "Ordinance of '87," so often spoken of. . . . In 1803 we purchased what was then called Louisiana, of France. It included the present States of Louisiana, Arkansas, Missouri, and Iowa; also the Territory of Minnesota, and the present bone of contention, Kansas and Nebraska. Slavery already existed among the French at New Orleans, and to some extent at St. Louis. In 1812 Louisiana came into the Union as a slave State, without controversy. In 1818 or '19, Missouri showed signs of a wish to come in with slavery.

what is now the State of Missouri, was settled in part by Slaveholders. And when that territory, according to the law, gave notice that they should apply for admission into the Union, the North voted that she should not be admitted unless she framed a State Constitution excluding involuntary servitude, and they were the majority. Neither the North nor the South would yield, and the discussion became angry and endangered the peace of the Union. A compromise was made by agreeing that all territory bought of the French, north of 36°30′, should be free, which secured the whole of Nebraska, Iowa and Minnesota to freedom, and left the balance of the French purchase south of the line to come in as free or not, as they might choose to frame their state Constitution.

Missouri chose to come in a slave-state, and was so admitted, as was afterwards Arkansas, according to the compromise. And afterwards, when first the Democrats and afterwards the Whigs held their Conventions at Baltimore, in forming their platforms they

This was resisted by Northern members of Congress; and thus began the first great slavery agitation in the nation. This controversy lasted several months, and became very angry and exciting,—the House of Representatives voting steadily for the prohibition of slavery in Missouri, and the Senate voting as steadily against it. Threats of the breaking up of the Union were freely made. . . . At length a compromise was made, in which, as in all compromises, both sides yielded something. It was a law, passed on the 6th of March, 1820, providing that Missouri might come into the Union with slavery, but that in all the remaining part of the territory purchased of France, which lies north of thirty-six degrees and thirty minutes north latitude, s l a v e r y should never be permitted. This provision of law is the "Missouri Compromise." . . . It directly applied to Iowa, Minnesota, and to the present bone of contention, Kansas and N e b r a s k a. Whether there should or should not be slavery south of that line, nothing was both declared that compromise to be a "finality," as to the subject of slavery, and the question of slave territory was by agreement settled forever.

There was no more agitation of the subject till near the close of our war with Mexico, when three millions were appropriated with the design that the President might purchase territory of Mexico, which resulted in our obtaining possession of California, New Mexico, and Utah. This was new territory, with which Jefferson's provision and the Missouri Compromise had nothing to do. The gold in California led to such a rush of immigration that that territory soon became filled with the requisite number of inhabitants, and they formed a constitution, and requested an admission into the Union. But the South objected because her constitution excluded slavery. This gave rise to the "Wilmot proviso," no more slave territory; next the "Omnibus bill," and finally what are called the "compromise measures of 1850," which comprised among other things the following:

said in the law. But Arkansas constituted the principal remaining part south of the line; and it has since been admitted as a slave State, without serious controversy. . . .

Preceding the presidential election of 1852, each of the great political parties, Democrats and Whigs, met in convention and adopted resolutions indorsing the compromise of '50, as a "finality," a final settlement, so far as these parties could make it so, of all slavery agitation. . . .

But going back a little in point of time. Our war with Mexico broke out in 1846. When Congress was about adjourning that session, President Polk asked them to place two millions of dollars under his control, to be used by him in the recess, if found practicable and expedient, in negotiating a treaty of peace with Mexico, and acquiring some part of her territory. . . . In the spring of 1848 a treaty of peace was made with Mexico, by which we obtained that portion of her country which now constitutes the Territories of New Mexico and Utah, and the present

1st. The "fugitive slave law," which was a concession on the part of the North to the South.

2nd. California was admitted as a free State, called a concession of the South to the North.

3rd. It was left with New Mexico, and Utah to decide when they became States, whether they would be free or not. This was supposed by the North to settle the question of slavery in this new territory, as the question with regard to the former territories had been settled forever.

The matter with regard to slavery was now settled, and no disturbance could be raised except by tearing up some of the Compromises with regard to the territory where it was already settled. The South had got all they claimed, and all the territory south of the compromise line had been appropriated to slavery; they had gotten and eaten their half of the loaf of bread; but all the other half had not been eaten yet; there was the extensive territory of Nebraska secured to freedom, that had not been settled yet. And the slave-State of California. . . .

In the fall of 1848 the gold-mines were discovered in California. This attracted people to it with unprecedented rapidity, so that on, or soon after, the meeting of the new Congress in December, 1849, she already had a population of nearly a hundred thousand, had called a convention, formed a State Constitution excluding slavery, and was knocking for admission into the Union. The proviso men, of course, were for letting her in, but the Senate, always true to the other side, would not consent to her admission, and there California stood, kept out of the Union because she would not let slavery into her borders. . . . A compromise was finally effected. The South got their new fugitive-slave law, and the North got California (by far the best part of our acquisition from Mexico) as a free State. The South got a provision that New Mexico and Utah, when admitted as States, may come in with or without slavery as they may then choose. . . . After an angry and dangerous controversy, the parties made friends by holding power attempted to snatch that away. So on Jan. 4, 1854, Douglas introduced the famous Nebraska Bill, which was so constructed before its passage as to repeal the Missouri Compromise, and open all the territory to the introduction of slavery. It was done without the consent of the people, and against their wishes, for if the matter had been put to vote before the people directly, whether that should be made a slave territory, they would have indignantly voted it down. But it was got up unexpectedly by the people, hurried through, and now they were called upon to sanction it.

They ought to make a strong impression against the imposition; that would prevent the consummation of the scheme. The people were the sovereigns, and the representatives their servants, and it was time to make them sensible of this truly democratic principle. They could get the Compromise restored. They were told that they could not because the Senate was Nebraska, and would be for years. Then fill the lower House

dividing the bone of contention. The one party first appropriates her own share, beyond all power to be disturbed in the possession of it, and then seizes the share of the other party. It is as if two starving men had divided their only loaf; the one had hastily swallowed his half, and then grabbed the other's half just as he was putting it to his month. . . .

On January 4, 1854, Judge Douglas introduces a new bill to give Nebraska territorial government. He accompanies this bill with a report, in which last he expressly recommends that the Missouri Compromise shall neither be affirmed nor repealed. . . . About a month after the introduction of the bill, on the judge's own motion it is so amended as to declare the Missouri Compromise inoperative and void. . . . In this shape the bill passed both branches of Congress and became a law. . . . Keep it [slavery] out until a vote is taken, and a vote in favor of it cannot be got in any population of forty thousand on earth, who have been drawn together by the ordinary motives of emigration and set-with true Anti-Nebraska members, and that would be an expression of the sentiment of the people. And furthermore that expression would be heeded by the Senate. If this State should instruct Douglas to vote for the repeal of the Nebraska Bill, he must do it, for "the doctrine of instructions" was a part of his political creed. And he was not certain he would not be glad to vote its repeal anyhow, if it would help him fairly out of the scrape. It was so with other Senators; they will be sure to improve the first opportunity to vote its repeal. The people could get it repealed, if they resolved to do it.

tlement. The Missouri Compromise ought to be restored. For the sake of the Union, it ought to be restored. We ought to elect a House of Representatives which will vote its restoration. . . .

But it is said we cannot restore it; that though we elect every member of the lower House, the Senate is still against us. It is quite true that of the senators who passed the Nebraska bill, a majority of the whole Senate will retain their seats in spite of the elections of this and the next year. But if at these elections their several constituencies shall clearly express their will against Nebraska, will these senators disregard their will?

Every point made in the speech, of course, was not reported in the Bloomington paper. The high point of the address was made when Lincoln, referring to the Bill of Douglas which was indifferent to the spread of slavery in the new territory, said:

This declared indifference, but, as I must think, covert real zeal, for the spread of slavery, I cannot but hate. I hate it because of the monstrous injustice of slavery itself. I hate it because it deprives our republican example of its just influence in the world; enables the enemies of free institutions with plausibility to taunt us as hypocrites; causes the real friends of freedom to doubt our sincerity; and especially because it forces so many good men among ourselves into an open war with the very fundamental principles of civil liberty, criticizing the Declaration of Independence, and insisting that there is no right principle of action but self-interest. . . . I particularly object to the new position which the avowed principle of this Nebraska law gives to slavery in the body politic. I object to it because it assumes that there can be moral right in the enslaving of one man by another. I object to it as a dangerous dalliance for a free people—a sad evidence that, feeling prosperity, we forget right; that liberty, as a principle, we have ceased to revere.

II

LINCOLN'S AUTOBIOGRAPHY

The text of his Autobiography which Lincoln sent to Jesse W. Fell on December 20, 1859, as copied from a facsimile, is as follows:

I was born Feb. 12, 1809, in Hardin County, Kentucky. My parents were both born in Virginia, of undistinguished families—second families, perhaps I should say. My mother, who died in my tenth year, was of a family of the name of Hanks, some of whom now reside in Adams, and others in Macon counties, Illinois. My paternal grandfather, Abraham Lincoln, emigrated from Rockingham County, Virginia, to Kentucky, about 1781 or 2, when, a year or two later, he was killed by indians, not in battle, but by stealth, when he was laboring to open a farm in the forest. His ancestors, who were quakers, went to Virginia from Berks County, Pennsylvania. An effort to identify them with the New England family of the same name ended in nothing more definite than a similarity of Christian names in both families, such as Enoch, Levi, Mordecai, Solomon, Abraham, and the like.

My father, at the death of his father, was but six years of age; and he grew up, litterally [*sic*] without education. He removed from Kentucky to what is now Spencer county, Indiana, in my eighth year. We reached our new home about the time the State came into the Union. It was a wild region, with many bears and other wild animals still in the woods. There I grew up. There were some schools, so called, but no qualification was ever required of a teacher, beyond *"readin, writin, and cipherin"* to the Rule of Three. If a straggler supposed to understand latin happened to sojourn in the neighborhood, he was looked upon as a wizzard [*sic*]. There was absolutely nothing to excite ambition for education. Of course when I came of age I did not know much. Still somehow, I could read, write, and cipher to the Rule of Three, but that was all. I have not been to school since. The little advance I now have upon this store of education, I have picked up from time to time under the pressure of necessity.

I was raised to farm work, which I continued till I was twenty-two. At twenty-one I came to Illinois, and passed the first year in Macon county. Then I got to New Salem, at that time in Sangamon, now in Menard County, where I remained a year as a sort of Clerk in a store. Then came the Black Hawk war; and I was elected a Captain of Volunteers —a success which gave me more pleasure than any I have had since. I went [through] the campaign, was elated, ran for the Legislature the same year (1832) and was beaten—the only time I ever have been beaten by the people. The next, and three succeeding biennial elections, I was elected to the Legislature. I was not a candidate afterwards. During this Legislative period I had studied law, and removed to Springfield to practice it. In 1846 I was once elected to the lower House of Congress. Was not a candidate for re-election. From 1849 to 1854, both inclusive, practiced law more assiduously than ever before. Always a whig in politics, and generally on the whig electoral tickets, making active canvasses. I was losing interest in politics, when the repeal of the Missouri Compromise aroused me again. What I have done since then is pretty well known.

If any personal description of me is thought desirable, it may be said, I am, in height, six feet, four inches, nearly; lean in flesh, weighing, on an average, one hundred and

eighty pounds; dark complexion, with coarse black hair, and
grey eyes. No other marks or brands recollected.

Hon. J. W. Fell.   Yours very truly,

A. Lincoln

III

THE REPUBLICAN NATIONAL CONVENTION OF 1860.

In addition to the accounts of the Chicago Convention
by Leonard Swett and Jesse W. Fell, which have been
quoted, there are some interesting sidelights on the proceedings which help to explain Lincoln's nomination in
the face of the tremendous odds against him. It was almost a foregone conclusion that William H. Seward, of
New York, would be nominated, and to defeat him it took
real adroitness on the part of Lincoln and his managers.
Edward Judd, for many years a lawyer, first in Chicago
and later in Seattle, was a son of Norman B. Judd who
made the nominating motion for Lincoln in this famous
Convention. Many years later in a conversation with
Rufus Rockwell Wilson, Mr. Judd told of his father's
part in the preliminary arrangements.

When in the late winter of 1860, said Mr. Judd, Mr. Lincoln returned to Illinois from a trip to New York and the
New England States, in the course of which he had delivered
his historic address at Cooper Union, it was with a growing
belief that there was a fair chance that in the end he might
be the Republican nominee for President. Seward and Chase
then bulked largest in the popular mind, but there was a
possibility, so shrewd a politician as Mr. Lincoln was quick
to foresee, that they might kill one another off, when their
followers came to close quarters in the convention, and thus
the way be opened for him to secure Republican leadership
in the nation.

With such an outcome in mind, Mr. Lincoln, as soon as he

was back in his Springfield office, resumed in a quiet but effective way the work he had begun before his eastern trip to secure an Illinois delegation to the national convention, fully and definitely committed to his candidacy. My father was among the first to whom he sent letters. Early in February he had written my father in characteristic fashion that while he was in a position where it would not hurt much for him not to be placed on the national ticket, it would be harmful to him not to secure the Illinois delegates to the convention. 'Can you help me a little,' he concluded, 'in your end of the vineyard?'

Our home was in Chicago, and Northern Illinois, the old Whig end of the state was strong for Seward. Nevertheless, my father was able to lend Mr. Lincoln prompt and effective aid. Not only did he see to it that a fair sprinkling of delegates from Northern Illinois to the state convention were favorable to his candidacy, but as a member of the national committee he succeeded in persuading that body to name Chicago as the meeting place of the national convention. Nor did this end his labors. Two or three days before the assembling of the convention on May 16, 1860, father returned home late at night, and, assuming that my mother was asleep, before he made ready for bed, quietly lighted a lamp on the table in the far corner of the room, and busied himself with pencil and paper.

At the end of half an hour, mother, who was awake, got out of bed and quietly crossed the room to discover what father was doing. As she approached his side, father, unconscious of her presence, remarked to himself:

'Egad, Abe's nominated.'

'What do you mean, Norman?' asked mother.

Whereupon, father, flourishing the sheet of paper on which he had been at work, delivered himself in this wise:

'The national committee met this afternoon and assigned to me the seating of the delegates in the convention, and, egad, Abe's nominated.'

Then father proceeded to give reasons for the faith that was in him. What he had been at work upon was a diagram of how he proposed to seat the delegates on the morrow. The state delegations committed to Seward he planned to seat in the front of the hall. Those favorable in whole or in part to Lincoln's candidacy were to have seats in the center. To the delegates supporting other candidacies than those of Seward and Lincoln or still in doubt as to how they would vote, he assigned whenever possible the rearmost rows of seats. Thus, when the balloting began, the Seward men would be isolated from the groups of delegates last named, while the supporters of Lincoln would be ideally placed for missionary work among them. Father's plan was followed without change of any sort, and with the results he had jubilantly predicted to my mother. Seward led on the first and second ballots, but thereafter steadily lost ground, while such good use did the Lincoln men make of the opportunity father had shaped for them that their candidate gained seventy-odd votes on the second ballot, and on the third carried off the nomination with a round hundred votes to spare.

Although Leonard Swett, in his letter describing the Chicago Convention, from which I have quoted, states that "no pledges have been made" by the Illinois managers, the conviction is growing stronger as time goes on that pledges *were* made in at least two instances. The day before the nomination Lincoln had written to his managers: "Make no contracts that will bind me," but he was in Springfield, reasoned Davis, and could not know the situation they faced in Chicago. Accordingly it is quite likely that the support of the Indiana and Pennsylvania delegations were obtained for Lincoln in return for promises that Caleb B. Smith and Simon Cameron should be given cabinet positions by President Lincoln. When the Convention was over Lincoln declared: "They have gambled on me all around, bought and sold me a hundred times. I cannot begin to fill the pledges made in my name." On the other hand, we have the following report of a conversation Thurlow Weed had with Lincoln during December, 1860:[1]

[1] Weed, Thurlow, *Autobiography* (Boston 1883) p. 612.

In the course of our conversations Mr. Lincoln remarked that it was particularly pleasant to him to reflect that he was coming into office unembarrassed by promises. He owed, he supposed, his exemption from importunities to the circumstance that his name as a candidate was but a short time before the people, and that only a few sanguine friends anticipated the possibility of his nomination. "I have not," said he, "promised an office to any man, nor have I, but in a single instance, mentally committed myself to an appointment."

But even though there may have been some bargaining on the part of Lincoln's managers at Chicago, I think we may agree with Albert Shaw when he said: [1]

Doubtless there is some evidence that the Pennsylvania delegation was assured that Mr. Cameron would be considered for a high position, and the same thing may have been true of Caleb Smith of Indiana, and one or two others. There was no lack of adroit management, but it would be overstraining minor details to assert that Lincoln's nomination had been brought about by deliberate bargaining. The gradual development of his strength as a political leader in Illinois sufficiently accounts for his nomination, when the tide had turned against Seward.

Chance and another piece of adroit work by Lincoln's friends combined to make their leader's success assured. It was chance which gave them the opportunity—the failure of the printer of the tally forms to deliver them to the Wigwam late in the afternoon of the second day of the Convention (Thursday, May 17, 1860) in time to vote on the nominations. If the Convention had remained in session on that day, it is not unlikely that Seward would have been nominated on the first or second ballot. As it was, the Convention adjourned until the next morning by motion of an unknown delegate, and thus

[1] Shaw, Albert, *Abraham Lincoln: a Cartoon History.* 2 vols. (New York 1929) vol. ii, p. 67.

Lincoln's men were allowed a margin of time of which they took full advantage. In order to indicate just how close a margin the Convention failed to nominate on the second day of its meeting, I will quote from the end of the official proceedings for that day:[1]

Mr. [Aaron] Goodrich, I move that we adjourn. [Cries of "No," "No," "Ballot," "Ballot."] I withdraw the motion, and move that we now proceed to ballot for a candidate for the Presidency. [Applause.]

Mr. [Benjamin] Eggleston, I renew the motion to adjourn.

The motion to adjourn was put and lost.

Mr. R. M. Corwine, I move that we now proceed to ballot for President. [Great disorder, and cries of "Ballot," "Ballot."]

Mr. [D. K.] Cartter, I call for a division by ayes and nays, to see if gentlemen want to go without their supper. [Derisive laughter, and cries of "Call the roll."]

The Chair—I am requested by the Secretary to inform the gentlemen of the Convention that the papers necessary for the purpose of keeping the tally are prepared, but are not yet at hand, but will be in a few minutes.

A voice—I move that this Convention adjourn until ten o'clock to-morrow morning.

The motion prevailed, and the Convention adjourned until ten o'clock to-morrow morning.

Ward Hill Lamon, Lincoln's local Bloomington law partner at this time, sized up the situation, and has left to us his version of what followed:[2]

There was a large delegation of roughs there for Mr. Seward, headed by Tom Hyer, the pugilist. These, and

[1] Republican Party, National Convention, *Proceedings . . . 1856, 1860 and 1864* (Minneapolis 1893) p. 142-43.
[2] Lamon, W. H., *The Life of Abraham Lincoln* (Boston 1872) p. 448.

others like them, filled the Wigwam toward the evening of the second day in expectation that the voting would begin. The Lincoln party found it out, and determined to call a check to that game. They spent the whole night in mustering and organizing their "loose fellows" from far and near, and at daylight the next morning "took charge" of the Wigwam, filling every available space, and much that they had no business to fill. As a result, the Seward men were unable to get in, and were forced to content themselves with curbstone enthusiasm.

The adroit work consisted in following out Lamon's idea of filling the Wigwam the next morning with Lincoln sympathizers to the exclusion of Seward men. I am indebted to Mr. Rufus Rockwell Wilson for the previously unpublished information that Alexander Hamilton Conner, of Indianapolis, was attending the Convention and interested in helping the Lincoln cause in any way that he could. It seems that the printer of the tickets of admission, a man named Hersey, was a former resident of Indianapolis and an old friend of Conner's. Through the intervention of Mr. Conner, Lamon was able to procure a large supply of extra tickets which, all through the night, were signed with the names of officers of the convention by a group of young men mustered for the purpose. These tickets were then distributed by the thousand to Lincoln men who filled the seats of the Wigwam long before the Seward sympathizers arrived at the usual hour after proudly parading through the streets of Chicago. Of course this was not strictly an ethical procedure, but I suppose the Lincoln men felt justified because of the high-handed methods of the Seward men the day before as described by Lamon above.

The year 1860 was before the days of long and elaborate nominating speeches, which were instituted during the 1876 Republican National Convention by Colonel Robert G. Ingersoll. Lincoln was nominated by these simple short statements, which are recorded in the official record:[1]

Mr. [N. B.] Judd, of Illinois, I desire, on behalf of the delegation from Illinois, to put in nomination, as a candidate for President of the United States, Abraham Lincoln, of Illinois. [Immense applause, long continued.] . . .

Mr. C. B. Smith, of Indiana, I desire, on behalf of the delegation from Indiana, to second the nomination of Abraham Lincoln, of Illinois. [Tremendous applause.] . . .

Mr. [Columbus] Delano, of Ohio, I rise on behalf of a portion of the delegation from Ohio, to put in nomination the man who can split rails and maul Democrats—Abraham Lincoln. [Great applause.] . . .

Mr. [W. M.] Stone, of Iowa, Mr. President, I rise in the name of two thirds of the delegation of Iowa, to second the nomination of Abraham Lincoln. [Great applause.]

Lamon and Conner, from their seats on the platform, lead the tremendous cheers of the Lincoln followers upon each mention of their leader's name. Then the balloting began to determine who should be the nominee of the Convention for the presidency. On the first ballot Seward lead with 173½ votes, Lincoln had 102 and Cameron trailed with 50½ votes. On the second ballot Seward had 184½, Lincoln 181 and Cameron had two. Chase of Ohio came third with 42½ votes. On the third ballot, Seward lost with 180 votes and Lincoln gained with 231½—but 1½ votes less than the 233 necessary for the choice. An Ohio delegate then announced a change of four votes from Chase to Lincoln, and Lincoln became the nominee of the Convention with 364 votes.

A few days after the Chicago Convention Henry J. Raymond, Editor of the *New York Times*, wrote an account of his impressions of the Convention, which was published in his paper.[2] He indicated how important

---

[1] Republican Party, National Convention, *Op. cit.*, p. 148-49.
[2] *New York Times*, May 24, 1860.

he held the shouts of the Lincoln men to be for the successful nomination of Lincoln in these words:

The nomination which it [the Convention] finally made was purely an accident, decided far more by the shouts and applause of the vast concourse which dominated the Convention, than by any direct labors of any of the delegates. . . . I mean by this that down to the time of taking the first ballot there had been no agreement among the opponents of Seward as to the candidate upon whom they should unite. The first distinct impression in Lincoln's favor was made by the tremendous applause which arose from the ten thousand persons congregated in the Wigwam, upon the presentation of his name as a candidate,—and by the echo it received from the still larger gathering in the street outside. The arrangements for the Convention were in the hands of Mr. Lincoln's friends, and they had been made with special reference to securing the largest possible concourse of his immediate neighbors and political supporters. It was easy to see that the thundering shouts which greeted every vote given for him, impressed what Mr. Greeley calls the "ragged columns forming the opposing host" with the conviction that he was the only man with whom Mr. Seward could be defeated.

Mr. Raymond wrote merely as an observer, however, for we have seen that Lincoln's nomination was not an accident. Lincoln heard about the part played by Mr. Conner, probably from Lamon, and sent to the former a cordial note of thanks, a fact which has not hitherto been published.

INDEX

Ames, Charles Gordon, 103-04, 127, 130.
Angle, Paul McClelland, 70n, 98n, 122n; quoted, 44n-45n.
Anti-Nebraska Meetings, 39-43, 45, 57-59.
Autobiography, Lincoln's, 98-100, 173-75.

Baddeley, ———, 8-9.
Barton, William Eleazar, 1, 10, 99n, 104n-105n; quoted, 2.
Beveridge, Albert Jeremiah, 1, 21, 32n, 70n, 83.
Bloomington Republican Convention, 60-69.
Burnham, John H., quoted, 101-02, 144-46.

Chicago Republican Convention, 110-17, 175-82.
Codding, Ichabod, 103; letter to, 50-51.
Conner, Alexander Hamilton, 180-82.
Crothers, Eli K., lawsuit of, 54-56.
Crothers, Lulu M., quoted, 56.
Crothers, Rachel, 56n, 57.

Davis, David, 4, 7, 12, 14-15, 19-22, 24, 32, 35, 52, 55-56, 65n, 67, 74-75, 88-90, 95, 98, 99n, 100, 102, 110-12, 115-16, 123-26, 128-29, 135-39, 140, 146, 153, 160-61, 177; quoted, 147-51.
Decatur Republican Convention, 108-10.

Dickey, Theophilus Lyle, 38, 65n, 152.
"Discoveries and Inventions," Lecture on, 78-79, 101-02.
Douglas, Stephen Arnold, 36, 42, 44-49, 51, 59-60, 69, 83-87, 89-95, 97, 136, 152, 171.

"Editorial Convention," 57-58.
Eighth Judicial Circuit, 9-15, 19-21, 29, 52-53, 74, 128.
Emancipation Proclamation, 131-34.
Ewing, James Stevenson, 32n, 89, 127; quoted, 42, 48-49, 116-17.

Fell, Jesse W., 3-4, 6-7, 47-48, 68, 79-80, 87, 89, 102-04, 127, 134-35, 161-62, 173-75; quoted, 44-47, 94-98, 115-16; letter to, 99-100.
Fell, Kersey H., 5, 53-54, 95, 102-03, 130, 145.
Fifer, Joseph Wilson, 77; quoted, ix-x, 89-90.
Fleming, Samuel G., lawsuit of, 54-56.
Free Congregational Society, 102-04.

Gridley, Asahel, 4-5, 64.

Herndon, William Henry, 14, 21, 32, 36, 59, 69, 70n, 135, 151; quoted, 66-67, 76-77.
"House Divided" Speech, 38, 64-65, 81-82, 152.